Shopping Brake

Proven tips to stop shopping wrong, and start shopping right for a wardrobe you love

Lisa Deerwood

This book is a work of nonfiction. The author of this book does not dispense medical advice. The intent of the author is only to offer information based on views, opinions, and personal experiences. In the event you use any of the information in this book for yourself, the author assumes no responsibility for your actions.

Visit the author's website at: shoppingbrake.com

Cover illustration and design by Britta Nagy

Interior illustration and design by Britta Nagy

Editing by Kelly Hogate

Table of Contents

Introduction

Why I wrote this book and how to use it

Have you ever had a closet meltdown moment, a time when you found yourself sitting on the floor with your clothes haphazardly strewn about as you cried out, "I have nothing to wear!" Have you ever purchased something new and then tried to hide it from your spouse or significant other? Have you ever owned a piece of clothing that you loved but struggled to style it into an outfit? Have you ever gotten stuck while attempting to clean out your closet? Have you ever found yourself running late because you spent too much time agonizing over what you were going to wear? Have you ever stood in a room full of people and felt that everyone around you was well put together, except for you? Have you ever looked inside your closet and grown so frustrated that you felt like just "giving up"?

These questions are merely examples of the challenges and consequences that we face from shopping mindlessly. But how do you shop intelligently? And is it really possible to own a wardrobe filled with things that you not only love, but actually use? Yes it is, and I'm going to explain how.

Throughout this book I'm going to guide you through the multiple things that you can do to shape your current wardrobe into something you love. But why should you listen to me? Because one of the biggest hurdles in my life was compulsively shopping for clothes, and I had the large, unorganized, chaotic mess of a closet and personal style to prove it. I always felt that I never had anything to wear, yet my closet was bursting at the seams. In a vain attempt to bring peace and order to my wardrobe I spent countless hours editing, organizing, then re-organizing my closet. I regularly shopped both at the mall and through the internet, misled by the notion that all I had to do was buy the perfect item and my wardrobe woes would be no more. Despite all of my efforts to improve my wardrobe, I continued to leave the house feeling like I had failed. The harder I tried to fix my problem, the farther away I seemed to move from the solution.

Over time I became addicted to shopping, and all of the non-working time in my life was solely dedicated to fueling my obsession with my clothes. I hit rock bottom before the lightbulb went off. I might have a shopping addiction but I also had an edge of my own: I've worked as both a researcher and a scientist. That is a very powerful combination. The terms researcher and scientist are often linked together—research scientist—but these are actually complementary skill sets. A researcher is an investigator, someone who studies something to better understand the facts. A scientist is someone who critically looks at a problem and then solves it empirically, using the scientific method to answer questions in a measurable way.

As a professional research scientist I have spent years examining problems and finding solutions, then processing the information so that the results mean something to an outside audience. This book contains the results of my personal research, with myself as the test subject. I've practiced every tip in this book, and they were essential factors that helped me walk along the pathway to success. Now I shop both smarter and faster, I'm no longer addicted to shopping, and I own a wardrobe that I love. And you can too.

How To Use This Book

This book is organized with each chapter containing action steps that lead you to one end goal: loving your wardrobe. How you choose to use this book is entirely up to you. If you are looking to reinvent how you shop for and manage your wardrobe, and you have a little extra time to spend, begin with Chapter 1. The early chapters help you lay a foundation upon which you will re-shape both your shopping behavior and your wardrobe. If you are interested in learning more about a specific feature about shopping and managing your wardrobe, or you are pressed for time, simply jump to the topic that interests you the most and continue from there. You can always revisit the rest later.

No matter which option you choose, you have a companion by your side. Throughout this book I highlight my personal experiences, both the highs and the lows, to act as your guide as you work towards your final destination—becoming the grand master of a wardrobe that you love. Within each chapter you will also find tips, labeled *Hit The Brakes*, which explain what to do and how to do it. These tips have been designed so that you can assemble a wardrobe that fulfills the needs of your current lifestyle, thus ensuring that you will own a closet filled with clothes that you not only love, but actually use as well.

Chapter 1 focuses on identifying your shopping behavior. Are you really addicted to shopping? And if you are, just how bad is it? You won't be able to measure your progress if you don't know what your baseline value is— the benchmark to compare to.

Chapter 2 examines your closet, helping you to break down your wardrobe into all of its individual parts. You have to know how much you have spent and what you already own, so that you can start figuring out what is causing your wardrobe woes. Here you will also learn what a wardrobe capsule is, how many of these you actually need, and how large each one should be.

Chapter 3 helps you to declutter the obvious items from your closet first. Here you learn the basic steps to figuring out what things you no longer want or can use. In doing so, you will no longer suffocate underneath the weight of unused clothing, or be forced to view the physical evidence of your past shopping mistakes.

Chapter 4 keeps your closet edit moving forward by helping you figure out how much you really need to own to be happy with your wardrobe. You'll learn what you really wear, what you don't, and how to get rid of the excess without feeling bad about it.

Chapter 5 shifts the focus from your closet to your personal style. You aren't ready to shop until you know what will work for you. With this goal in mind, you learn the answers to questions regarding what styles you prefer, as well as what silhouettes and colors will have you looking and feeling your best.

Chapter 6 outlines a few tools that you can use to help guide you and ensure that you stay focused when you go shopping. Through shopping lists, plans, and worksheets, you'll increase your chance of walking away having bought items that are just right for you, while staying clear of making costly mistakes.

Chapter 7 discusses the factors that lead to impulse shopping and why willpower alone is not strong enough to bring about a change in shopping behavior. The act of shopping is broken down into small tasks so that you can practice until your new behavior becomes second nature. The benefits of receiving support and guidance from others while you are seeking changes to the way you shop are also covered.

Chapter 8 examines the steps you can take to ensure that the wardrobe you've customized for yourself continues to function well over the long term. The importance of paying attention to what you keep, as well as what you add to your wardrobe, is covered, along with how to do it.

Chapter 9 highlights why a person relapses when trying to change bad habits and addictive behavior. It reveals the triggers and common strategies employed by retailers to spark you to buy when you don't really want to. By learning what outside influences encourage you to shop, you can shield yourself from becoming a target and ensure that you don't go on a spending spree unintentionally.

Chapter 10 is filled with wardrobe challenges to remind you of the most important feature to owning a wardrobe: having fun with it! All of the hard work that you've been putting in is finally able to pay off in the best way possible—providing joy. Wardrobe challenges help keep your wardrobe feeling fresh and new, while stretching your creative muscles.

Final Words

This book exists because I am someone who struggled with and ultimately conquered compulsive shopping. Inside these pages I've outlined every step that led to my success. Changing your behavior and educating yourself on how to own a wardrobe that you love is not an overnight event. It's a process, containing a series of steps that build on each other, rising upward until you reach your end goal: mastery of your wardrobe. To truly become an expert on your wardrobe requires hard work, dedication, and patience. Success will not happen overnight, and it's not always going to be easy to stay focused on the end goal. But if you decide to commit to making a change, and you don't give up no matter how difficult the task seems, you'll never look at your wardrobe, or shop for clothes, the same way again. And you'll be glad that you made the change.

Chapter 1

Honey, you have a problem

It's time to admit that
something has to change

If I were to ask you the question "are you a shopaholic" how would you answer it? Yes or no? Now how confident are you that the answer you just gave me is the correct one? In the "make believe" worlds from books and movies, a shopaholic is portrayed as a fashionista with a bubbly personality. A superficial person who is obsessed with acquiring the latest clothes and shoes. A woman whose impulsive behavior causes her to get in over her head, but that's OK because by the end of the tale the heroine has staged a successful comeback, walking away with her life better off than when the audience first met her. But real life is not like the movies, and clinical research paints a very different picture of someone who is suffering from a shopping addiction.

The death of a spouse or loved one, unemployment, divorce, parenthood, retirement—these life-altering circumstances may plunge a person into a state of despair, spurring them to seek solace in shopping. Other times, initiation into the club of shopaholics is not clear cut, there is no life-altering circumstance that compels the individual to shop. Instead the troublesome behavior starts small, almost unnoticeably, and it's not until considerable time has passed, that the evidence grows too large to be ignored. My foray into shopping addiction and amassing a large, non-functional wardrobe didn't begin with some grandiose moment, it began with small steps. In addition to purchasing the items that I needed, I occasionally started tossing in just one little extra thing to my pile of must-haves. Perhaps on one trip that extra item would be a top that I didn't need but I rather liked anyway. On another visit it might be an extra pair of shoes because they were on sale and I fancied the color.

As time passed, the practice of adding in additional, random items to my pile of purchases eventually became second nature to me. Even worse, shopping for clothes, shoes, and accessories was incorporated into my daily life. Shopping escalated from once a month, to once a week, to once a day or more. Eventually I didn't even realize that I was shopping anymore, it was just another part of my daily routine. I bought so much and so often that I was on a first-name basis with the FedEx man, the UPS guy, and the sales associates from my favorite brick and mortar stores. I could tell you when a window display or mannequin on the sales floor was changed and spot from across the room which pieces were the latest merchandise from among an overcrowded sales rack. To support my shopping addiction, my handbags grew in size. The bigger the bag, the more items it could hold, thus allowing me to carry new purchases into my home without the telltale evidence of a store shopping bag. And when my tote could no longer handle everything that I purchased, I simply hid it all in the trunk of my car until I could "sneak" my stuff into the house without anyone noticing. I would cut off the tags and mix the new garments in with my older clothes, confident that by mixing the 2, no one would be able to spot the difference. Other times I would leave the tags on and shove the clothes off to the side, because I wanted to make sure that I always had something new hanging inside my closet to look at. If someone inquired about something that I wore, I never revealed the true retail price or when I actually purchased it—I lied. I didn't want anyone to think that I was spending too much or shopping too often, because I knew deep down that what I was doing was wrong. Does any of this sound familiar? If it does, rest assured that you are not alone.

The constant longing for new items is not something that many people can escape. In 2013, a study published by Müller A, et al, in the *American Journal of Addictions*, reported that roughly 7% of the US population, about 20 million American consumers, suffer from some form of compulsive buying. And this number has risen sharply over the past 20 years.[1] Even worse, among people who were diagnosed with a compulsive shopping disorder, a follow-up interview 5 years later revealed that only

[1] Müller A, Mitchell JE, de Zwaan M. Compulsive buying. *Am J Addict*. 2015;24(2):132-137.

18% of people felt that they had successfully quit their compulsive shopping.[2]

With the large number of people afflicted with compulsive shopping behavior, how is someone who is staring into their closet declaring that "I have nothing to wear" supposed to know if the disorganized collection of clothes and shoes in front of them is a) evidence of a shopping addiction or b) merely the result of poor shopping habits? And with the low rate of success in behavior change, if you are a shopaholic, how do you regain a sense of control, and, more importantly, how do you make the new habits stick over the long term? Identifying compulsive shopping behavior is the focus of this chapter. In the rest of this book I'll give you the tools to help you reshape then maintain a wardrobe that is perfect for you.

It's not always simple to spot a problem. When someone is falling into debt, living in a hoarding environment, and/or is unable to pay for the roof over their head or their day-to-day bills, it's easy to label that person as someone who is living with a shopping problem. But there is also another type of shopping addict: the person who has money in their bank account, room to move freely in their home, and is able to pay their bills on time. Which brings about an important question:

**Is it still a problem when you can
actually afford what you purchase?**

[2] Black DW, Shaw M, Allen J. Five-year follow-up of people diagnosed with compulsive shopping disorder. *Compr Psychiatry*. 2016;68:97-102.

Sometimes, the answer is yes. For some folks, their initiation into the realm of shopaholics is the direct result of small steps that happen over an extended time period. A person who is addicted to shopping does not always live in a hoarding-style situation and struggle to pay their bills; sometimes an overshopper simply shops and owns more than they can use. And when the signs are subtle, and you have advertisers telling you that it's admirable to be a fashionista, it becomes very easy to ignore the notion that you even have a problem. I was one of those people. My closets were overstuffed, but I could still walk freely throughout my home, and my day-to-day bills were always paid on time. If this sounds like you, then you don't have the blatant signs that you are addicted to shopping. Which means that you are going to have to do a little investigating to 1) identify if you truly do have a shopping problem, and 2) establish a baseline of how bad it is, so that you can measure your progress over time. Before you can start gathering the facts and making changes, you have to understand the act of shopping itself and know the difference between *compulsive* and *impulsive* shopping.

I'm going to start with the easy one first. The difference between *compulsive* and *impulsive* shopping is planning. Someone who shops *compulsively* has thought about shopping for a long time and attempts to rationalize it; the action of shopping was pre-meditated. A shopaholic is always thinking about what to shop for, when to shop, how to shop, and reviews their performance from past shopping trips. On the contrary, someone who shops *impulsively* doesn't think about the shopping experience; the purchase is made on instinct alone, the action of shopping was not pre-meditated. Everyone succumbs to impulsive shopping at some point in their lifetime—sooner or later you are going to see something in a store, want it, and walk out of there with it in your hands.

Thus far, I have covered 2 types of shopping, with the distinction being planning—yes (compulsive) or no (impulsive). But, wait just a minute, wouldn't that mean that everyone who thinks about what they are going to buy is a compulsive shopper? No. The act of shopping itself revolves around 4 key elements:

1. Purchase frequency
2. Browsing time
3. Money spent
4. Emotional motivation

The impulsive shopper spends little or no time with each of the 4 key elements of shopping—they hit the gas pedal and speed right through. A person addicted to shopping hits the brake pedal often during their journey, their set of rituals forcing them to spend a considerable amount of time with one or more of these areas. Which brings me to the first of many *Hit The Brakes* tips in this book.

Hit The Brakes:

Knowing the 4 key elements of shopping tells you what behavior(s) you need to change, if any

When you know what your problem areas are among the 4 key elements of shopping, you have armed yourself with a very powerful piece of information. Black and white numbers don't lie. Through your own research you can prove, with cold, hard facts, whether you are addicted to shopping. And if you already know that you are a shopaholic and you want to change your behavior, pinpointing your problem areas among the 4 key elements of shopping will tell you which key element (or elements) you will need to change, and you will have a baseline value to compare your progress against over time. To guide you on how to gather this information, I'm going to focus on the key elements of shopping one at a time, using myself as the case study so that you have an example to follow while you collect your own data. Are you ready to put on your lab coat and begin your experiment? Then let's get started.

Key Element of Shopping #1—Purchase Frequency

Experts in psychology and addiction blame online shopping for the rise in compulsive spending. I don't disagree. Online shopping can act just like crack cocaine for a shopaholic. You see an outfit on a model that you want, and armed with a credit card and the click of a button, it's all yours. The shift from traditional in-store shopping to online shopping is supported by a recent survey by the United Parcel Service, which reported that in 2016, 44% of smartphone users made purchases from their device, an increase of 14% from the previous year.[3] It's easy to track how often you make a purchase and to monitor your progress over time. Every time you walk away from a retailer with a bag in your hand or a receipt from an online order waiting in your inbox, you've made a purchase. That's your purchase frequency—data on how often you shopped.

To monitor my purchase frequency I used a calendar and marked every time that I shopped and at what stores I made a purchase over a 1-month period. I also recorded the number of days between shopping trips, keeping in mind that shopping can be done both in person and online. When I began my data collection I had a sneaky suspicion that I might be shopping too often, but I wasn't ready to believe that this gut feeling was trying to tell me that I was addicted to shopping. The only way to convince myself that I was overshopping was to look at some cold, hard evidence. An example of my monthly calendar is below (Figure 1).

[3] United Parcel Service. 2016 UPS Pulse of the Online Shopper. Available at: https://pressroom.ups.com/pressroom/ContentDetailsViewer.page?ConceptType=PressReleases&id=1465390876904-365. Accessed on: September 23, 2016.

Figure 1: *Purchase Frequency—1-Month Summary*

Sunday	Monday	Tuesday	Wednesday	Thursday	Friday	Saturday
1 1	**2** 2	**3** 3	JCrew 4	**1** 5	**2** 6	**3** 7
Nordstrom 8	**1** 9	**2** 10	**3** 11	Express 12	**1** 13	**2** 14
Calvin Klein Aerosoles 15	Clarks 16	Macy's 17	**1** 18	**2** 19	**3** 20	The Limited 21
JCrew 22	Nordstrom 23	BCBG Express 24	**1** 25	**2** 26	Rockport 27	**1** 28
Cole Haan 29	**1** 30					

I marked every day I went without a purchase with a number **(in bold)**, counting up as I progressed. For each day that I made a purchase, I recorded the name of the store(s). If I made a purchase, I started the count over the next day. After the first month, I realized that I hadn't gone more than 3 days without making a purchase! My eyes widened as I shook my head. That couldn't be right. I decided to track for a second month. I repeated the process, making a note of the days and retailers when I made a purchase, and counting the number of days in between. For month 2, I went up to 4 days without making a purchase! This was nuts, and starting to make me mad. So I tracked for a third month and the outcome was even worse, only 2 days! It ended up taking me 4 months to acknowledge that I was shopping too often.

Once I finally realized how often I was shopping, I entered a state of denial. After all, a few months of shopping a lot doesn't necessarily mean that I have a shopping problem, right? Maybe it was just a couple of bad months? I was certain that I could stop at any time. So I decided to play a little game. How long could I go without buying something? I began with a small step. My goal was to go 1 day longer than the previous month before making a purchase. For example, if I only went 3 days without making a purchase for a particular month, then the next month I would try to go 4 days without making a purchase. The month after that, 5 days. Piece of cake, right? Wrong! The longest I went without buying something for my wardrobe was 30 days. I would always crack after 30 days.

In the example above (Figure 1), I bought something for 12 out of the 30 days for the month. That meant I shopped for 40% of the days within 1 month. Not only did I shop for almost half of the month, but I also did not go even a single week without making a purchase. That's an awful lot of shopping!

The insights that I gained from tracking my shopping habits didn't stop after I realized how often and where I was making purchases. I learned something else as well: the impact that my high frequency of acquiring new items had on my wardrobe. Let's go back to the example figure again (Figure 1). If I purchased only 1 item at the conclusion of each shopping session, I would have added 12 new items to my wardrobe within 1 month. If I repeated my shopping habit for the second month, I would once again have added 12 new items to my wardrobe within a 30-day period. This means within 2 months, I would have made purchases 24 out of 60 days, once again 40% of the time. And I would have added 24 new items to my wardrobe within this time period. So what would happen to my wardrobe if I continued my shopping habit for 6 months? If I maintained this shopping pattern for 6 months, I would have shopped on 72 days and added 72 items to my wardrobe. That's an awful lot of new stuff. But wait, because there's more. If I repeated this behavior over 1 full year, I would have shopped on 144 days and added a total of 144 pieces to my wardrobe. Yikes!

If you like to shop as much as I did, analyzing your shopping frequency will show you how your closet, which was once well-organized and functional, can quickly become unmanageable and overcrowded, in a very brief period of time. Even worse is the fact that these numbers are often higher in reality. Why? How often do you really purchase only *one* thing during a shopping trip? I know I rarely did. I typically bought lots of stuff every time, often forsaking quality items for quantity. The more stuff I brought home, the better. After all, why should I spend $100 on 1 thing, when I can spend $100 and walk away with 10 items instead? If you don't know how often you are shopping, recording your purchase frequency will answer this question. And if your numbers look anything like mine did, then you are probably shopping too often and purchasing too much, which is evidence that you are addicted to shopping.

Key Element of Shopping #2—Browsing Time

Discovering how often on a monthly, weekly, and even daily basis that you buy is very helpful, but that is only 1 of the 4 elements of shopping. You also have to figure out the total amount of time spent during each shopping trip, regardless of whether you made an actual purchase or not. To figure this out, you repeat the monthly tracking exercise above, except this time you log the number of visits and the length of time you spend browsing. The outcome of the shopping trip itself doesn't matter, it is the time that is of interest here. The hours, minutes, and seconds throughout the day that involve "just taking a look." All instances of shopping are included: physically wandering the aisles of a brick and mortar store, surfing via the web or an app on a smartphone, and perusing goods from a home shopping program on television. If you want to figure out where you stand with the second key element of shopping, browsing time, then every time that you are looking for something to buy, you must record the time.

How do you know if you spend too much time shopping? Well, let's take a look at the day of a shopaholic. The first day that I tracked how much time I spent during each of my shopping visits, I discovered 2 things: 1) I had browsed a total of 5 times, and 2) each individual session ran for 45 minutes. That's right, on 5 separate occasions during a single day I not only thought about shopping and searched for something to buy, I also wasted almost 4 hours doing so! Even worse, none of these instances involved physically visiting a retail store. Apparently, anytime I was near a computer or smartphone, and had free time, I browsed.

Online browsing was a large contributor to the total time I allocated to shopping, but it was not the only way that I shopped. I was frequently sneaking in shopping sessions in person too. In fact, monitoring my browsing habits revealed a huge obstacle I would have to overcome if I ever wanted to break my addiction to shopping—my lunch break. My lunch hour provides a prime opportunity to step away from the hustle and bustle of the office, allowing me to recharge for the afternoon. And my favorite place to spend my lunch hour was at the local mall.

During those lunchtime shopping trips, it was not only very easy but also quite tempting to purchase a "pick me up item." And while the pick me up item could be anything that would make me feel good—a cup of coffee, a new lipstick, a fashion magazine—more often than not, my pick me up item was something for my wardrobe. Lunchtime shopping had a second perk—the short time frame dedicated to shopping was exhilarating. On these lunchtime shopping excursions I often felt like I was a participant on a game show. As I parked my car and walked to my destination, I could almost hear the host talking beside me as they addressed the group.

"Alright contestants, let's line up."

My heart rate would quicken and my breathing would become fast and short.

The host continued. "Contestants, you have 45 minutes to find the best deal possible."

My muscles would tense in anticipation of the host's next words.

"Ready. Set. Go!"

And I would be off! A woman on a mission, I entered the store with only one goal in mind: to buy something! The pressure to find and to purchase something within a 45-minute timeframe was both frustrating and exhilarating. For those 45 minutes I could shed the mild-mannered office worker persona. I was the lioness, searching for her prey on the Serengeti plains of Africa. There was no time to waste. I had to act smart and move quickly. In those 45 minutes my only goal was to locate the best deal possible, and then snatch that elusive item up for myself, before time ran out. With a successful hunt under my belt, I would be ready to return to the office, energized and eager to complete the second half of my workday.

Daily lunchtime shopping was a significant contributor to the total amount of time I spent browsing and shopping every day. And, these lunchtime shopping expeditions had a side effect I didn't anticipate, but should have. The small daily purchases impacted not only the time I spent shopping, but also affected the size of my wardrobe. Lunchtime wardrobe additions are like snowflakes. An individual snowflake is pretty, and fun to observe as it falls from the sky. On its own, the snowflake has little impact on its surroundings. The same can be said for purchasing a single item during a shopping trip. One item has little impact on the size of one's wardrobe. When a snowflake is part of a blizzard, now that's a different story. The once charming and special snowflake is simply one of thousands, maybe even millions, and snowflakes in those numbers wreak havoc. Blizzards can shut down a city for days as roads wait to be cleared. With no proper place to be stored, the leftover mounds of snow become a nuisance, as it can take days and sometimes weeks to fully melt.

Are you a lunchtime shopper too? Let's take a look at the impact this can have on someone's wardrobe. Remember the effect that overshopping had on my wardrobe when we were looking at shopping frequency (the 144 pieces I would have purchased over 1 year). Well, the same effect occurs when purchasing lunchtime items. One $10 T-shirt purchased once a week, turns into 52 new T-shirts added to my wardrobe over the course of a full year. And the total spent from these additions is $520! The clothes and money spent sure add up fast, don't they? Reducing this amount by half can have an impressive impact on your wardrobe and your budget, but it will still leave its mark. If you are a shopaholic, then you already know how hard it is to go shopping and to try not to buy anything. Consider this, if you shop on your lunch break like I did, even if you managed to resist buying something during half of your shopping trips, your wardrobe would still end up with an additional 26 new T-shirts, and you would have spent $260, solely from items purchased during those 45-minute safaris during your lunch hour.

And lunchtime shopping had a third pitfall. It is rushed shopping. After all, I needed to get back to work. This left me with having to make on-the-spot decisions, and often left no time to try on the item before checking out. The shopping time was spent on selecting something I liked, paying for it, trying it on at home, and often returning it the very next day so that I could purchase something else. Most bad behaviors fall into a routine, and my lunchtime shopping was no different. Every day of the week became dedicated to focusing on the offerings from retailers and what was in my wardrobe. Monday would be return day for the weekend purchases, Tuesday was to scope out the stores, Wednesday was the day to buy because my favorite retailers would usually have sales on Wednesdays, Thursday would be another return day, usually for the Wednesday items, Friday would be another purchase day because the weekend is here. That meant that Saturday and Sunday were also return days.

Equally as damaging to both my budget and my free time was shopping from the confines of my own home.

Even at home, away from the stores and despite staying away from my computer or smartphone, I didn't rest from shopping. I own a TV, and televised home shopping channels were always my channel of choice. I would leave the TV on as "background noise" while cooking, cleaning, and especially when eating. And in doing so, I was once again exposing myself to lots and lots of temptations.

Monitoring your browsing time will reveal how much of your time each day you dedicate to shopping. And along the way you just might uncover your biggest contributor to damaging your wardrobe. For me that was lunchtime shopping. The new additions that I purchased on my lunch break improved my mood, but also brought multiple consequences. I inadvertently increased the size of my wardrobe, while also igniting my desire to constantly revisit retailers to make returns, which would then lead to yet more purchasing. If you often complain that you do not have enough spare time to exercise, clean the house, cook meals at home, spend time with friends or family, or participate in a hobby, and you are addicted to shopping, part of the problem might be because you are spending all of your free time on browsing and ultimately buying new stuff.

Key Element of Shopping #3—Money Spent

The first half of the key elements of shopping is now complete. You know how often you buy something new for your wardrobe (purchase frequency) and you are aware of how much time you spend during each of those shopping sessions (browsing time). With this knowledge you are now ready to move on to the 2 more personal and harder to identify key elements of shopping: money and motivation.

Money is one of those topics that has 2 sides. Often someone either justifies or complains about money. When justifying, the talk centers around receiving a pat on the back for saving money. "This only cost me $5 after coupons." "I saved $10 using my store credit card." "I got this item on the sale rack for half off." When complaining, the talk is focused on getting reassurance that it was OK to spend the money. "I can't believe I spent $300 on these boots." "I purchased that coat full price and I don't even wear it." "This dress was expensive, but I needed it for a wedding." When the conversation turns to money, the discussion revolves around either how much one saved or how much one spent. No matter which angle you use, your end goal is the same: you want your audience to reassure you that the money you paid had been a wise decision.

At first glance, tracking how much money you spent at the end of a shopping trip sounds like it would be easy. Grab a notebook, jot down the date, place, and total amount spent, add up the totals at the end of a month, and presto, you'll know how much money you've shelled out for new things. However, it didn't take long for tracking how much I was spending to turn into a real mess.

In fact, this step was the most work for me, because many shopaholics, including myself, are serial returners.

Figure 2: *The Behavior of a Serial Returner*

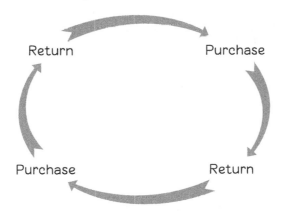

A serial returner is someone who chronically returns items (Figure 2). As a serial returner I was never satisfied with my purchases. I bought a few items, returned them to the retailer a short time later, and left having purchased additional new items. My habit of constantly purchasing and returning made it very difficult to track how much money I was really spending. And it came with an unexpected side effect—my serial returner behavior was very time consuming. Not only was I visiting the stores to make a purchase, but I was also motivated to re-visit the retailer to make a return.

To track how much money I was spending, I used an accounting ledger. This is typically a green, 6-column pad that you can find in an office supply store (or an EXCEL spreadsheet could work too). An example of 1 month and year to date spending entry is below (Table 1). Purchases are in black, returns are in **bold**. The far right column tracks the total per month. At the end of the year, I would figure out the average that I spent.

Table 1: *Summary of 1 Month and Year to Date Spending*

	Monthly Spending				Yearly Spending	
Date	Store	Purchase Total	Return Total			Monthly Totals
April 4	JCrew	$314.00			January	$256.00
April 8	Nordstrom	$159.00			February	$33.54
April 9	JCrew	$150.00	**$127.05**		March	$1075.68
April 11	Express	$49.98			April	$1381.40
April 12	Express	$24.99	**$24.99**		May	
April 15	Calvin Klein Aerosoles	$55.69 $75.00			June	
April 16	Clarks	$115.00			July	
April 17	Aerosoles Macy's	$85.00 $15.13	**$75.00**		August	
April 21	Nordstrom The Limited	$202.00 $89.97	**$159.00**		September	
April 22	JCrew	$98.00	**$58.00**		October	
April 23	Nordstrom	$124.62	**$79.50**		November	
April 24	Express BCBG	$10.55 $156.00	**$24.99**		December	
April 27	Rockport	$95.00				
April 29	JCrew Cole Haan	$98.00 $110.00	**$98.00**			
Monthly Total		$2027.93	**$646.53**		Year to Date Total	$2746.62

The first time I tracked my monthly and yearly spending, my average came to $549.00 per month! I was stunned. I must have made a mistake. With 12 months in a year, that monthly amount equals $6,588 a year on my wardrobe! And if I kept up my shopping and spending habits for 5 years, I would have spent a total of $32,940.

For 10 years, $65,880. I could have bought a Mercedes for that kind of money!

The realization that I was literally spending thousands and thousands of dollars on my wardrobe was sickening. Spending all of my money on shopping meant that I was unable to use that money for anything else. And the return on my financial investment was zero. My clothes were not going to increase in value, most of what I purchased was not vintage or designer labels. The items were not going to sell for more than I purchased them. In fact, my clothes were not even making me happy. Many of the items I just "had to have" left me frustrated because I could not assemble an outfit with them. I never felt happy about my daily looks. And yet I kept on shopping, spending, and remaining frustrated with my wardrobe. Uncovering how much money you're spending can be the wake-up call that you need to realize that your shopping addiction is preventing you from achieving your financial goals, and is something that you have to change.

Key Element of Shopping #4—Emotional Motivation

With 3 quarters of the elements of shopping puzzle completed—how often you purchase items, how much time you spend shopping, and how much money you have been spending—only 1 piece remains for you to finish your work to discover what your shopping behavior looks like: emotional motivation. The first 3 elements of shopping were number based, making data collection easy. But emotions are not based on numbers, which makes this element of shopping the hardest to track and the most difficult to change. For now, we are going to focus on establishing the emotional reason for your shopping. Later on in Chapter 7 I'll discuss why emotional shopping is so difficult to change, and how to do it successfully.

In today's society, the emotional motivation to shop is encouraged repeatedly and often. We are surrounded by opportunities to browse and purchase items. In the United States and many other industrialized countries, such as the United Kingdom, France, Germany, and Japan, shopping has extended beyond brick and mortar stores to online store fronts as well. Shopping is easier to do than ever before, and it's always available. Pair the emotional motivation to shop with the ease and accessibility of shopping, and it's easy to see how shopping can turn into an addictive behavior. But what exactly is emotional motivation and why do emotions lead to overshopping?

Emotional motivation:
The mind-body connection leading to overshopping

In psychology, emotion and motivation are often studied together because emotions and motivation demonstrate a cause and effect relationship; emotions move a person to act. When considering someone who is addicted to shopping, the person often shops because they have been emotionally motivated to do so. The overshopper feels a strong desire to do something (motivation) and acts out this strong desire by shopping. Shopping itself results in physiological responses (changes in chemical secretions, heart rate, blood pressure, etc) for the shopper and these changes are linked to emotions (happy, sad, angry, etc). The behavior of a shopaholic is similar to that of someone addicted to drugs, alcohol, or gambling—their body becomes chemically imbalanced and only the act of shopping will restore the equilibrium (Chapter 7 will discuss this in detail). The difference in chemical imbalances between one brain and the next is why everyone does not react the same way to an identical situation.

As a shopaholic, I was motivated to visit a store because I wanted to shop, not because I actually needed something for my wardrobe. And once I bought something, I had an emotional response: my new purchase left me feeling happy, sad, etc. Because I was often emotionally motivated to shop, the feelings that arose from shopping did not quench my desire to shop; instead they fueled it. If the act of shopping were a burning fire, the emotional payoff from shopping was the extra pile of kindling added to the fire, it kept me shopping. For someone who is not an overshopper, they are driven to visit a store because of a need or desire for a specific item. The emotional payoff from purchasing something is not strong enough to spark another flame to shop again; instead it is like dumping a bucket of water on it, the flame sputters out and the desire is gone.

For an overshopper, shopping feeds the fire.
For a non-overshopper, shopping quenches the fire.

Figuring out what emotions are driving your behavior to shop means that you have to take your analysis inward and look at yourself. What feelings are serving as the kindling and feeding the fire? It's not fun to analyze your feelings, but it is an essential part of why you are shopping too much and why you feel that you cannot stop. So how do you figure it out?

To identify my emotional motivations for shopping, every time I found myself in a store (either in person or online) I asked myself one simple question: "Why?" More specifically, "why am I here?" Once I got into the habit of asking myself "why" while I was at a store, I reframed the question. Before I got in my car and drove to a store I would ask myself, "why am I going?" After answering that question became part of my routine, I reframed the question again. This time my target was my time on the checkout line. When waiting in line to make a purchase I asked, "why am I buying this?" In the beginning, it was not easy to remember to ask myself "why" every time I shopped. I would often forget to ask myself "why" until I had already arrived at home long after the high of a new purchase had worn off.

It became necessary to plant physical reminders to myself. These prompts helped to re-mold my behavior, so that I could incorporate asking myself "why" as a natural part of my shopping routine. Eventually I placed a note with the word "why" wrapped around my credit card in my wallet. A second note was added to the collection of reminders on the monitor of my computer at work. More than once I found myself reaching for my credit card, to stumble upon the note with the word "why." When I saw that note, I would have to step out of line while I answered the question (in my head of course). In the end, inquiring "why" became a habit, and a pattern began to emerge. If you are a shopaholic too, the emotional motivations for constantly shopping can be grouped into 3 large buckets: escapism, re-invention, and acceptance.

Emotional Motivation for Shopping—Escapism

Shopping was my favorite way of taking a break from my everyday life. Shopping served as a distraction, providing an activity that allowed me to ignore the unpleasant and boring areas of daily living. And, unlike some of the other vices in life that may have negative associations—smoking, drinking, gambling—shopping is generally viewed as a positive activity. Unless someone knows that you are struggling with a shopping addiction, they probably won't have a negative comment if you admit what you have done. A little shopping is a socially acceptable activity.

As a socially acceptable activity, escapism through shopping can be divided into 2 forms: self-suppression and self-expansion. Self-suppression escapism arises from a focus to avoid the negative. When I had a tough day at work, no problem, I'll just stop at the mall to unwind. An argument with a friend, no worries, I'll just swing by a store and browse. Bored while waiting for dinner to reheat, no big deal I can always peruse the latest deals on the web. Self-expansion escapism stems from the need to execute the positive through immersion in the activity. Browsing and shopping were my rewards for doing a good job at work, achieving a personal fitness milestone, or any joyous event in my life. Big or small, the reason itself did not matter. I could express my good fortune with a little shopping and purchasing.

Self-suppression escapism: "I am feeling negative today."
Self-expansion escapism: "I am feeling positive today."

It didn't matter if the feelings were good or bad, shopping was the means to avoid the negative areas of my daily life, and the avenue to acknowledge the positive areas too. Shopping became my outlet for my emotional state. With shopping, I could release the emotional tension that built up during my daily life. By asking yourself "why," you will discover the real reason you visit a retailer, and if you do so because your real goal is to lift yourself up or to put yourself down, then shopping and buying are the means to an end.

Emotional Motivation for Shopping—Re-invention

Clothes are one of the ways that we portray our inner selves to the outside world. The successful entrepreneur, the homemaker, the fashionista, the hippie chick—

through your clothes, you show the person you want other people to see. But when you aren't happy about something in your life, you are going to try to seek a way to change it, and one of the options is through re-inventing yourself with your clothes. You shop because you want to take up a different way of life.

When my underlying goal was to re-invent myself, I became a chameleon, trying on different personas for each of my passing moods. Walking down the sidewalk, I saw a woman that looked stunning in her ensemble. She was attired head to toe bohemian style. Deciding I wanted the same carefree nature, I would begin to study the features of the boho look. After my crash course, I would run to the stores with the intent to adopt the boho style for my very own.

On a particular day, I may have sported an outfit by one brand. The ease of assembling the outfit, and the coordination of the pieces, left me with the idea of working with a specific brand as a way to simplify my shopping. How easy it would be to shop at only one store all the time and always look put together. I could become "That woman in head to toe [insert brand name here.]" So I would narrow my focus, studying the evolving collections of a specific retailer over a given time period. Even when I didn't like the current collection, I would try to force myself to find at least something, because I was only going to shop from that one brand.

I would wear a scarf 3 days in a row and decide I could become known as "that woman in the scarf," and off for more scarves I would go. I would read about French minimal wardrobes and decide that I wanted a French wardrobe so that I could be "Parisian chic" too. Back to the stores I would hurry, seeking out those essential Parisian wardrobe pieces. Coming up with ways to re-invent myself left me feeling empowered. I could become anyone I wanted to be, even if it was for only a limited amount of time.

I really enjoyed these shopping sessions. It felt like I was playing dress up for adults. Anything that was a style outside of my normal look was fair game. I would try on everything that caught my eye, because "you never know until you try." These shopping trips were not only about re-invention, but also experimentation. I could try on a new persona for a short while, even if it was only for as long as I stood alone in the dressing room. I wasn't satisfied with who I was. Heck, I couldn't even tell you who I was, so I kept trying out new versions of me. The boho gal, the prepster lass, the sporty chick, the arty girl. As I struggled to develop an identity for myself, my wardrobe increased in both size and variety. It didn't take long for my closets to become filled to the brim, a schizophrenic compilation of clothing and accessories that reflected my multiple fashion personas. One never knew how I was going to dress next. I had accumulated an outfit for every fashion style and every personal mood.

I could dress for any occasion, because I owned an outfit for each of them. Yet, despite the abundance and variety within my wardrobe, I was left feeling more confused than ever. And I still had nothing to wear. If any of this sounds familiar, then there is a high probability that your wardrobe has not only too much stuff, but also lots of different styles. A little variety can be nice, but when you have too much, it becomes overwhelming, and that could be one reason why you stand in front of your closet claiming that you have nothing to wear. If this is like you, don't worry, because in Chapter 5 I'll provide tips to help you figure out your personal style.

Emotional Motivation for Shopping—Acceptance

Shopping to re-invent yourself and shopping for acceptance are often used interchangeably. While these 2 things can happen at the same time, they are not the same thing. A woman who just started a new job after years of sitting in classrooms earning her degree will find herself shopping for 2 reasons at once. She needs a wardrobe to show the world she is working now (re-invention), and she needs to make sure that the clothes she's wearing to work fit in among her co-workers (acceptance). When you shop to re-invent yourself, you are shopping to create a new you; in the case of the new grad she is shopping for a business woman persona. When you shop for acceptance, you are searching for those magical key pieces that allow you to join the group; going back to the case of the new grad she is also shopping so that her clothes mimic the rest of her peers, so that she will gain access to the social groups at work.

I recently read the latest top 10 list for the season. Realizing that I didn't have enough of the "it" items, I went off to the mall. I want to join the ranks of women who are always current with their style. A co-worker comes into work and shows off her latest designer bag. I rush out to buy one too because I want her to see me as a designer bag wearing comrade. "Look at the 2 of us, we both carry designer bags."

Often people are very concerned about being accepted by others, but the person who is the hardest to please is usually yourself. I know for me it is. Most of the time, I am shopping and buying because I am trying to silence my biggest critic—me! And this is the one critic that I have to face every day—their presence is constant and their displeasure is relentless. When the jeans I wore today were feeling a smidge too tight, it is immediately time to pick up a new pair after work. If the red shade of that sweater is too warm for my skin tone, I'll be off to select a new one as soon as I am able to. I've developed a sudden desire to feel more feminine, then it is time to purchase more skirts and dresses. I really liked the feel of that silk top against my skin, I went shopping for more. Whenever I was not feeling satisfied with myself, shopping became my way of boosting my self-esteem.

At its highest level, shopping falls into 2 buckets: 1) I need this, or 2) I need to fill a void. A shopaholic typically owns lots and lots of clothes, spanning a wide variety of styles and colors, yet often feels like they don't own anything they can wear. The reality of the situation is that you own plenty of things, they just don't give you the emotional payoff any longer.

Every one of us is a unique individual. Innate differences mean that one person's reason for shopping is going to be different when compared with the next person. However, the underlying motivations are the same. The person is shopping with the goal of fulfilling a self-perceived need: a need to escape, a need to re-invent oneself, or a need to feel accepted.

Owning an abundance of clothing, yet feeling that you constantly need more, means that you have to do a little inner soul searching. Before you can address the problem, you have to discover why you are shopping in the first place. What are the voids you are trying to fill? You can't fill these voids in a non-shopping way until you understand the emotional motivations.

When I first mentioned the fourth key element of shopping, emotional motivation, I highlighted the usefulness of asking yourself "why" you are visiting a store. Returning to the why question, I grouped the reasons for shopping into the 3 buckets of emotional motivation: escapism, re-invention, or acceptance. Using myself as the lab rat, here is an example of the common statements that came up during my shopping and where they fall among the 3 emotional motivations to shop:

1. **Escapism:** Tough day at work. argument with a friend, bored waiting for dinner, reward for completing a task
2. **Re-invention:** Top 10 list item, signature style item, special event/occasion
3. **Acceptance:** Jeans make me feel sexy, color of top will get me noticed, everyone else has one of these

At first you may find that every time you ask yourself "why" you are in the stores you have a different answer. For myself, it took months for me to start to see the patterns. I wasn't just a style chameleon, I was also a shopping chameleon. Some days I shopped to fill a hole in my life or to relieve bad feelings. Other days I shopped like a woman possessed. I paid no attention to the prices or quantity, I merely shopped to maintain the "high" or good feelings that I had. And at other times, I shopped with a quest for perfection, because with the perfect items, I myself could become perfect.

Shopping was my outlet for everything I was trying to figure out about myself. With shopping I was able to escape (negative) or reinforce (positive) feelings. My wardrobe allowed me to express myself in a way that I couldn't figure out with words or other activities. Shopping gave me the outlet to experience self-reflection, re-invention, and creative expression. Unfortunately, the results were always short lived. It would not be long before I would repeat the walk down the pathway of a spending spree.

My addiction to shopping influenced my mental and emotional state, the size of my wardrobe, and my free time. But those weren't the only areas; other aspects of my life were affected as well. These included: finances, health, social interactions, and self-confidence. The financial impact of overspending is one of Hollywood's favorite ways to portray a shopaholic. Reports of people who are drowning in debt yet unable to stop themselves from shopping are common. Yet, this negative outcome does not end with the person who cannot afford their purchases. Even someone who can juggle their finances to accommodate both shopping and paying day-to-day bills is not immune to the negative implications of overshopping. Every purchase that someone makes, takes that money away from spending it on something else. Money that could be used to help a friend or family member in need, contribute to a charitable organization, or pay for a new hobby or a vacation is no longer available. The money that could have been used for something else is spent on material acquisitions instead.

The effect on one's health is one of the subtle side effects of a shopping addiction. The amount of time I spent on planning and physically shopping affected my sleep. I delayed resting in favor of online browsing. My nighttime ritual included hours of staring into the glare of the computer screen or tablet, perusing the latest goods.

I began to drink more caffeine to keep me alert and able to get through the day. One cup of tea became 2, then 3, progressing to 4 or more within a single day. I put off cooking food at home and grabbed something on the go instead, so that I could extend my shopping time. Three home-cooked meals per day were replaced with take-out. Eventually meals on the go were shoved aside, leaving protein shakes and candy bars as common daily food selections.

A person's social interactions suffer considerably from overshopping behaviors. Always eating on the go often means eating alone. Time spent over a meal at home with family members became a thing of the past, and I often brushed aside time to spend with friends in favor of shopping by myself instead.

The more I owned the less I seemed to use, leaving me wondering about my decision-making skills. I began to second guess every purchase. Shopping shifted from making me feel good about myself to filling myself with dread. Yet I continued to browse and shop. As a result, my closet continued to fill up and my wardrobe increased, along with my daily frustrations. Eventually I owned a closet filled with beautiful things that I didn't know how to put together into outfits. My attempt to fix the problem by buying something new left me angry, upset, and discouraged with myself. No matter how much time or money I spent, or how much or what I bought, I never seemed to amass a wardrobe filled with the right things for *me*.

If the behaviors of this chapter sound like you, then you are probably addicted to shopping. The rest of this book will present to you multiple ways to break free from your shopping addiction. Rest easy knowing that you are not alone, compulsive buying is a common problem. In 2004, a nationwide telephone survey of 2,513 adults reported that 5.8% of adults, more than 1 in 20, are affected by compulsive buying.[4] Some respondents reported that their uncontrolled shopping was a leisure activity, a way to express and manage self-identity, or a way to manage emotions. For others, shopping brought about severely negative consequences such as financial debt, strained relationships, and/or interference with one's workplace functioning.

The 4 elements of shopping—purchase frequency, browsing time, money spent, and emotional motivation—discussed in this chapter can be used to identify your problem areas. Once you know what your problem areas are, you will know what you need to change and you can use this information as a baseline to track your progress. As you work through these problems, you will find that shopping will no longer be a challenge for you.

The biggest culprit that ignites the urge to go shopping is often the closet itself. If you begin each morning inside your closet, struggling to select an outfit

[4] Koran LM, et al. Estimated prevalence of compulsive buying behavior in the United States. *Am J Psychiatry.* 2006;163:1806-1812.

to wear, there is a high probability that this unhappiness with both your outfit of the day, and what is sitting inside your closet at home, will cause you to spend much of your free time thinking about your wardrobe. If this sounds like you, keep reading, because in Chapter 2 we are going to set our sights on the closet itself, studying what is inside to understand why it is giving you a daily headache. I'll also discuss how to fix it so that when you look inside your closet in the future, you smile instead of frown. And you will always have something to wear.

Chapter 1 recap:

Before you can change your habits, first you must understand them.

 Hit The Brakes:
Knowing the 4 key elements of shopping tells you what behavior(s) you need to change, if any

- Use a calendar to track how often you make a purchase and how long you can go before you feel the need to buy something

- Jot down the amount of time you spend both in stores and online to see how much of your time you dedicate to shopping

- Record your purchase and return totals to track how much money you are spending

- Pinpoint your emotional reasons for shopping by asking "Why?" "Why am I here?" "Why am I going?" "Why am I purchasing this?"

Once you know where your problem areas are among the 4 key elements of shopping, you can start to change your ways, and you will have a baseline to compare your progress over time.

Chapter 2

You've got nothing to wear. Or do you?

Dissect your closet to understand your wardrobe

When you fantasize about your dream home, what features come to mind? A million dollar view? A huge kitchen? An infinity pool? A 10-car garage? My dream home has every one of these. Do you want to know what else my dream home has in it? An amazing walk-in closet. The crème de la crème of closets can be found in the houses and mansions of athletes, fashion designers, singers, movie stars, and other members of this elite group of people classified as the rich and famous. Their closets are huge, and have been designed with a heavy emphasis on organization and visibility—the owner's entire wardrobe arranged in neat stacks and perfectly ordered rows. With the additional touches of a comfortable place to sit, and some proper lighting, these dream closets are transformed from a space that is solely used to store clothing, to a place that is a personal sanctuary. There might be a lot of things inside, but these dream closets have been created to handle it all.

If you are reading this chapter, then it's a safe bet that your closet is similar to what mine used to be—exactly the opposite of a dream closet. Knitwear was stacked tall enough on the shelves to touch the ceiling, shirts were often double or triple layered onto a single hanger, and the closet rod held enough stuff for the sheer weight to cause the rod to bend to the point of almost snapping in half. Not only could I never find anything to wear, but I often discovered items that I forgot that I even owned! I've been startled awake in the middle of the night from shelving crashing to the floor. I've also witnessed a closet rod burst through the wall into another bedroom. Why were these crazy things happening to me? Simple, I owned too many things. If any of this sounds familiar, then at some point you have probably had the same thought as me: you own too much! And if you own too much stuff, well, then there is only one solution: you need to own a bigger closet, right? You couldn't be more wrong.

You see, increasing the size and number of closets and storage options in your home is not the answer to your problem. In fact, you can survive with a small closet or even none at all. Just ask anyone who is familiar with an older home and deals with this every day. Homes built before the 1900s often contained either a small closet or none at all. Back then, people didn't own a lot of items; therefore, closets weren't considered a necessary feature to include in a home. Go further back in time, and you'll discover that in the stone ages the first storage solutions were baskets, chests, and sometimes even tree trunks. These early creations were dependent on the materials available in the geographic region. Roman soldiers used simple wooden boxes to transport armor and weapons. During the late Medieval and Renaissance periods, low chests (or cassones) with elaborate carvings or paintings became popular. In addition to the storage of clothing or goods, the cassone was often used to carry the dowry goods for marriage.

As furniture construction methods advanced, so did the shape of the storage solutions. Chests were lifted off the ground, the opening was shifted from the top to the side, and shelves were added, thus creating armoires, cupboards, and wardrobes. It wasn't until modern times, when the popularity of owning and storing clothes increased, and building methods advanced again, that storage solutions became permanent fixtures in the home, and turned into the rod and shelf closets that you see today. When someone is out shopping for a house today, spacious, well-organized dream closets are often considered an envy-worthy feature.

Ok, so people can live without a big closet, that's great news, but I don't really care how people in the past managed to store their stuff. Besides, people didn't own a lot back then and I do. My problem is that my closet is a mess and I hate it. I want to own one of those celebrity dream closets.

Did you just nod your head? Does this sound like you? Because this complaint brings with it an important question: how do you shape your current closet into your dream closet? Well, let's take another look at those often coveted celebrity closets. What stands out about them, compared with the storage solutions of the past? A whole lot, actually. Yes, celebrity closets have all of that open space, the nice lighting, a chair or couch to sit on, sometimes even a nice chandelier. All of these features might make the closet something to be desired, but do you want to know what the most important characteristic is to owning a dream-worthy closet, instead of a cringe-worthy closet? The missing piece that links storage solutions of the past to you owning a closet that others will covet today is knowledge of what's inside.

At the end of the day, a closet is merely a spot in your home to store stuff, no matter how pretty its packaging is. If your closet is a constant source of frustration, leaving you wanting someone else's instead, that's because the closet that you have is no longer working for you. And yes, you can move out or hire someone to build a larger one, but do you really know what size you need? How about how many shelves should be inside? And should the closet rods be single or double stacked? You cannot shape your closet into the one of your dreams, until you know what you have inside, which is the focus of this chapter. Once you know this information, you can take the necessary steps to mold your closet into a personalized storage system that is perfect for you and you alone (Chapters 3 and 4).

Hit The Brakes:
Write down everything that is in your wardrobe

A popular proverb is the Latin phrase *"scientia potentia est"* which means "knowledge is power." Essentially, knowledge empowers you to obtain a result. In the case of working to create a dream closet you need to know 2 pieces of information about your wardrobe: what you own and how you use it. Figuring out what you own is very easy to do—simply write down everything that you have inside your closet. That's it. Just list it all on a piece of paper or an EXCEL spreadsheet. Sounds pretty simple, right? In fact, I thought that this step was so simple, that I didn't even have to do it. I mean come on, I know what's inside my closet, do I really have to bother to write it all down? Yes you do, you really do, and here's why.

When I prepared to move in with my husband, I had to pack up everything that I owned. And this included my wardrobe. In my old place, I had a reach-in closet with a shelf above the hanger rod. If only 1 or 2 sweaters were placed on the shelf, I could reach them unassisted. But to access my extensive collection of knitwear, I had to use a small step stool. I could not reach the items stored on the shelf unaided because the sweaters were stacked too high. And when the stacks of knitwear touched the ceiling, instead of taking that as a sign that maybe I owned a little too much, I simply began a new column of sweaters. Did I ever count them? No. Do you want to guess how many sweaters I had when I finally bothered to do so? Thirty of them. That's right, 30. If you own 30 sweaters, do you realize that you can go an entire *month* without repeating any of them even once? But wait, because there's more. Shocked at the high number, I forced myself to sit down and write down every single sweater that I owned. And what did I discover? Within that collection of 30 sweaters, I had at least one sweater for each color that was available during the past 2 retail seasons: black, gray, tan, wine, pink, purple, yellow, orange, green, navy, light blue, rust, ivory, and red. And within each color, there were multiple types of sweaters: pullovers, v-necks, turtlenecks, cowlnecks, boatnecks, cardigans, hooded, and off-the-shoulder styles.

I knew that I owned a lot of sweaters, but I never realized how many or how varied both for color and style my collection was until I wrote it all down on a piece of paper. Despite all of that variety, I realized there was a lot of repetition as well. After all, I didn't own 1 or 2 black sweaters, I had lots of them, each one in a different style. Realizing that I had 30 pieces of just one thing, sweaters, begged the question: just how big was my wardrobe? Bigger than I ever realized.

If you own a lot of stuff like I did, then writing down everything in your wardrobe will be a long, slow process, but if you persist, eventually you will be able to record every piece of clothing, footwear, handbags, and scarves that you own. Remember, when it comes to your wardrobe, you are the researcher, collecting the data (in this case what you own) so that later on, you will know what to do with it (what to save, what to donate, and what to purchase to make it work into outfits).

If you are listing out your wardrobe for the first time, I recommend that you create a separate tab in EXCEL (or simply use a separate sheet of paper) for each garment type: jeans, blazers, sweaters, cardigans, knitwear, blouses and shirts, trousers, shorts, T-shirts (long and short sleeve), scarves, boots, shoes, sneakers, etc. As you review what's in your closet, you can match up what you see with its appropriate category. When you own a lot of clothes, this task is going to be tedious and boring. I know it was for me. To prevent myself from becoming overwhelmed and discouraged I selected no more than 12 items at a time. Working with a small portion of my wardrobe and spreading out my task over the span of several days kept me on track and able to stay focused.

The first time I created a list of my wardrobe, I owned well over 300 items. It took me almost a month to compile the list. With 365 days in a year, I had enough variety to wear something new within each outfit for almost every single day for an entire year! This amount of variety did not leave me the time to repeat my favorite pieces. A portion of my original list is below (Table 2). I grouped items by category and color. Once you have this information you will be able to analyze it, just like a scientist collects data and then draws a conclusion.

Table 2: *Categorizing a Wardrobe by Item*

Category	Toppers		
Item	Blazers/Jackets	Sweaters	Cardigans
Color and Style	White Boyfriend Blazer	Dove Gray Crewneck	Black Crewneck
	Denim Jacket	Purple Cable Turtleneck	White Crop
	Black Boyfriend Blazer	Tan/Ombre Turtleneck	Black Sweatercoat
	Green Army Jacket	Red Cable Crewneck	Ivory/Black Print Boyfriend
	Black Moto Jacket	Black Cable Crewneck	Black Boyfriend
Total	5	5	5
Category	Bottoms		
Item	Jeans	Shorts	Skirts
Color and Style	Blue Straight Leg	Navy Twill	Blue A-Line
	Blue Bootcut	Denim Rolled Cuff	
	Dark Blue Bootcut		
	Cobalt Straight Leg		
Total	4	2	1

How do you analyze the data? Let's look at the blazers/jackets category from Table 2 for a moment. I have 5 blazers/jackets, of which 2 of them are the boyfriend style and 3 are the jacket style. If there are 5 days in a work week, I can wear a different blazer or jacket every day in the week. And for 3 of those days, I'll be wearing a jacket of some type. You know those times when you look at your closet and think that you have nothing to wear? Well, part of the reason may be because you are wearing too many of the same category of clothes. If I'm wearing jackets 3 days a week, I might get tired of them pretty fast. And if I'm wearing a blazer/ jacket 5 days a week, I might grow bored even quicker, because I am wearing outfits requiring me to layer all of the time. Need another example? Ok, let's move on to the cardigans category in Table 2. Once again I have 5 garments, this time 5 cardigans. Out of this group, I have 4 different styles (crewneck, crop, sweatercoat, and boyfriend) but 3 of them are the same color, black. Going back to that 5-day work week, I can wear a cardigan 5 days in a row and for 3 of them, I'll be wearing black. It's no wonder why someone can grow bored with their clothes, if you are wearing the same color all of the time, and you are a person who likes a little bit of variety, simply changing up the style of the garment, but not the color as well, will leave you feeling like you are not wearing anything different from one day to the next.

Creating a list, and analyzing it, was the first time that I realized that my wardrobe had way too much stuff. And not only did I own a large number of items, but many of these pieces were duplicates. Why on earth did I own 4 black skirts, when I don't even wear skirts? Or 15 pairs of bootcut jeans, when there are only 7 days in a week? And don't forget about those 30 sweaters—I still possessed enough knitwear to sport each item only 1 time per month.

Once you have a list of what you own, you can broaden your knowledge. For the second pass, you add an additional column, the purchase price. This new column will allow you to total up the entire cost of your wardrobe. If you don't remember what you paid for something, you can estimate it by looking up the current selling price of a similar item and using that number. When you tally up the total cost of your wardrobe you may be surprised by the final number. I know when I did this and I saw my total, my jaw hit the desk. I couldn't believe that I had spent literally thousands of dollars on clothes. An example table of item and cost is below (Table 3). With only 5 items in the table, the total cost is already over $500. It sure adds up fast, right?

Table 3: *Cataloging a Wardrobe by Total Cost*

Item	Cost ($US)
White Boyfriend Blazer	258.00
Denim Jacket	69.99
Black Boyfriend Blazer	99.90
Green Army Jacket	57.59
Black Moto Jacket	49.95
Total	**535.43**

Understanding how much you really own and how much you've spent can be a real eye opener. And if you are someone who is addicted to shopping, it might even give you a sinking feeling in your gut. I know the first time I saw the numbers, I almost cried. And a few clients of mine actually have cried. Why do some people have such a strong reaction? Because staring back at you is undeniable evidence that you are shopping too much and spending too much. Keep in mind that the amount of money that you have spent and the number of pieces that you own is from past shopping trips. How much you should actually own is a personal decision. What appears as too little to one person could be viewed as too much to someone else. Everyone's thresholds and budgets are different. There is no right or wrong answer here. One person may be satisfied owning a 400-item wardrobe worth $30,000 and another person can be happy with a 40-item wardrobe worth $1,500. There is no ideal wardrobe size or budget. Only you can decide for yourself what is the ideal number of items to own, and when the amount of money spent is enough. And the later chapters in this book will help you to figure it out.

If you don't like the numbers that you see, that's ok too, because now you know what you have done in the past. And since you are no longer clueless about what you have been doing, you can now start working on making changes so that you do not make the same mistakes again in the future. That is why "knowledge is power" when it comes to your wardrobe.

But why stop here, let's add a few more bits of information to your newly found knowledge about your wardrobe.

Hit The Brakes:
Pinpoint the number of
capsule wardrobes in your closet

One of the most popular phrases you will hear about clothes today is the phrase "capsule wardrobe" or sometimes the reverse, "wardrobe capsule." Originally coined in the 1970s, a wardrobe capsule is a collection of essential items, the pieces that form the core elements of a person's day-to-day wardrobe. Typically this collection of clothing consists of a small group of versatile items that function well together. A key feature of a small and successful capsule wardrobe is that all of the clothing mixes well together so that you can create a wide variety of outfits from a small number of pieces.

The popularity of capsule wardrobes has increased exponentially, driven by the consumer's desire for practicality. Often distilled down to a collection of 30 items, many bloggers currently discuss the "must haves" for a successful capsule wardrobe. The interest in capsule wardrobes has carried over into the marketing style of retail stores. It is not uncommon for a retailer to highlight "the essential 7-item wardrobe" when rolling out a collection for a new season. Advertisements of "12 items in 7 days" attempt to capitalize on the consumer's quest for multi-use clothing. Conversations on a Parisian woman's wardrobe, affectionately dubbed the "French capsule wardrobe," have become common. And no minimalist fashion blog would be complete without a discussion of a capsule wardrobe.

The concept of a capsule wardrobe is appealing, but how realistic is it? Some would argue not at all. Limiting oneself to a small collection of clothing can be seen as boring and too rigid. Others would disagree, stating the multiple benefits of a capsule wardrobe: less clutter, saving money, reducing consumerism, and gaining free space. The concept of a capsule wardrobe is often appealing, but putting the idea into practice can be challenging. The number one issue that I've noticed with capsule wardrobes is thinking that your entire wardrobe only contains 1 capsule. But you must remember that while a wardrobe capsule is a collection of clothes, it is actually many individual capsules that compose the entire wardrobe for most people.

Why does someone often have more than one capsule in their wardrobe? Because in today's society, people participate in more than one daily activity—sleeping, working, exercising, lounging, errand running, etc. Most likely your closet has many capsules within it, each one varying in size. Looking at my personal closet, I currently have 9 wardrobe capsules stored inside: formal work, casual work, weekend wear, loungewear, gear (horseback riding), sleepwear, workout wear, vacation wear, and special occasions. Additional capsules that a person may have include: travel wear, holiday wear, date nights, outer wear, intimates, accessories (handbags, jewelry, scarves, etc), and gear for activities such as gardening, hiking, bicycling, home renovations, theater, LARP, etc. The number and variety of capsules is based on your lifestyle, and the total number of wardrobe capsule inside a closet will be different from one person to the next. The more activities you participate in during your day-to-day life, the more occasion capsules you will require in your wardrobe.

To determine how many capsules are in your wardrobe, list all of the occasions that you participate in—family parties, working out, sleeping, lounging at home, business meetings, date nights, etc—over the course of 1 year. This list will show you the number of occasion capsules within your wardrobe. You may find this easier to do by reviewing each month on a calendar. To help you identify your occasions, below is summary of the occasions for each of my wardrobe capsules stored in my personal closet:

1. **Formal work:** Meets the needs of professional work settings, including formal business meetings and job interviews (suits, dresses, trousers, skirts, blouses, blazers, pumps)
2. **Casual work:** Informal, relaxed clothing that is suitable for casual work environments
3. **Weekend wear:** For running errands and doing chores around the house. A step down in style from casual work clothing
4. **Loungewear:** The clothes that you change into when you are not leaving the house and don't use to sleep in
5. **Gear:** This is usually a sport/activity-based capsule for activities done twice a week or less

(hiking, gardening, home renovations, theater, LARP, horseback riding, etc). When you don't have a lot of pieces, it's easier to group the clothes into one capsule

6. **Sleepwear:** What you sleep in
7. **Workout wear:** Clothes for running, biking, weight lifting, etc, if you do this activity often. Listing the clothes as a separate capsule makes it easier to manage the capsule. When you don't use these pieces often, keep them in the gear capsule
8. **Vacation wear:** Typical vacation clothes include beach wear and resort wear
9. **Special occasions:** Typical special occasions include engagement parties, weddings, funerals, bridal showers, and baby showers

Out of the 9 capsules in my wardrobe, my largest capsule is casual work. I usually wear these clothes 5 days per week throughout the year. In fact, this capsule is so large, it is further divided into 2 large groups based on the seasons, casual work—fall/winter capsule and casual work—spring/summer capsule. With this in mind, I technically have 10 capsules, but for the first analysis casual work wear will be kept as one capsule. Later on I'll go into more detail and break out this capsule by the 2 season groupings.

All of the occasion capsules in the list above are stored in my personal closet. However, they are not the only capsules in my wardrobe. Additional capsules that

I own include: outerwear, intimates, and accessories (scarves, jewelry, and handbags). These 3 capsules are not areas that I struggle to maintain for my wardrobe and are stored outside of my personal closet. Therefore, I didn't include them in the above list of occasion capsules.

Identifying the number of occasions requiring a capsule within your wardrobe moves you one step closer to understanding what is in your closet and helps you to acknowledge the events and activities that are, and are *not*, a part of your current lifestyle. You can better plan what to shop for and how much to own once you understand 2 things: 1) what capsules you need in your wardrobe and 2) how large each one should be. And speaking of size, this brings me to the next *Hit The Brakes* tip.

Hit The Brakes:
Figure out how often you need each occasion capsule in your wardrobe

I already told you that the number of wardrobe capsules that you own will be influenced by the number of activities in which you participate—the occasion capsules. The same is true for the size of the capsule itself. How often you participate in a given activity will affect how much stuff you have in each capsule. A wardrobe capsule related to an activity you participate in every day will naturally have more things in it than the wardrobe capsules for events that happen less often. When you know what the relative size of each wardrobe capsule should be, you will better understand how much you should keep or donate, when you edit your closet (Chapters 3 and 4).

Looking at the list you just created for the wardrobe capsules you need by occasion, mark the number of times that you will use each of your capsule occasions over 1 year. Then rate the capsules into one of 3 buckets based on the frequency of use: low, moderate, and high. Using my list from above, I have ranked the capsules into one of the 3 ratings (Table 4).

Table 4: *Determination of the Frequency of Use for Occasion Capsules Over 1 Year*

Occasion Capsule	Frequency over 1 year	Rating
Formal work	6 to 8 times per year	Low
Casual work	5 days per week, 50 weeks per year	High
Weekend wear	2 days per week, 52 weeks per year	Moderate
Loungewear	7 days per week, 52 weeks per year	High
Gear	2 days per week, 52 weeks per year	Moderate
Sleepwear	7 days per week, 52 weeks per year	High
Workout wear	5 days per week, 52 weeks per year	High
Vacation/Holiday wear	7 days per week, 2 weeks per year	Low
Special occasions	2 to 4 times per year	Low

This information can be used to decide how large or small an occasion capsule should be. Returning to Table 4, the low rated or least used capsules in my wardrobe are formal work, vacation/holiday, and special occasions. Both the formal work and special occasion capsules are only used a handful of times per year. The vacation/holiday wear capsule is used for a short period of time (2 weeks per year). The moderately used capsules are weekend wear and gear. These capsules are worn weekly, but only for 2 days per week. The wardrobe capsules in high demand include: casual work, loungewear, workout wear, and sleepwear. Items in these capsules are worn daily throughout the year.

When you have the itch to go out and do a little shopping, knowing which capsule you are shopping for will help you to decide what stores you should visit. If you want to add to your formal work capsule, you don't need to stop by a store that sells workout clothing and sneakers. For myself, my money isn't going to be well spent if I am purchasing lots of pieces intended for special occasions, since I rarely go to one. Recognizing the amount of use a capsule gets over the span of 1 year also forces you to face the reality of your current lifestyle. A cocktail dress might make you feel really good, but if you only have 1 event every year when you get to use it, well, I hate to burst your bubble, but you really don't need to shop for, nor own, more than 1 cocktail dress in your wardrobe. Sure, shopping for special occasion wear may be more fun, but adding clothes for your more often used wardrobe capsules is more practical. Understanding your wardrobe capsules can also help you when you are trying to streamline your closet. After all, you can't really decide what to keep or to donate for each capsule in your wardrobe until you understand how much you need. Although, if crunching the numbers in this chapter still leaves you uncertain as to exactly what these totals should be, don't worry, because Chapter 4 will help you to decide what should stay and what should be tossed when you get stuck editing your closet. Finally, understanding how often you use the pieces in your capsule wardrobes will help you to figure out how much to spend on something, by calculating the potential cost per wear of the item, which is covered in Chapter 6.

Hit The Brakes:
Study the color capsules
within your wardrobe

This chapter is centered on using the information that you gather from analyzing your own closet to learn your wardrobe preferences and needs. Thus far, I've explained how to figure out how many capsule wardrobes by occasion are in your wardrobe, as well as how much you should own within each capsule based on the anticipated frequency of use. Do you remember the reason why you started analyzing your closet in the first place? Because your closet, which is nothing more than a storage solution, has too much stuff in it. In Chapters 3 and 4, we are going to eliminate that problem. Before we can do that, there is another piece of information that will help you when you are deciding what to buy or what to donate, and it's also one of the reasons why you might find yourself standing in front of your closet complaining that you have nothing to wear.

Wardrobes that work well typically contain a well-balanced collection of colors. When the color capsules within a wardrobe are evenly proportioned, it is easy to assemble a matching outfit. Wardrobes that stray too far out of balance and contain hard-to-match colors, as well as too many or not enough basics, don't work. One of the reasons why you might think that you have nothing to wear is because you don't know what to do with what you already own, you are clueless how to put together an outfit. And one of the culprits causing your problem is the colors in your closet.

The colors within a wardrobe fall into 1 of 2 groups: color capsule or color accent. Color capsules apply when more than 1 item of the same color is found within the wardrobe; these are the colors often featured in your outfits. Color accents are used to identify the "wildcard" items within a wardrobe—when your wardrobe only contains 1 item of a specific color, this is a color you wear only sporadically.

How do you figure out your color capsules and color accents? Let's take a look at my wardrobe. My largest capsule, by occasion, is casual work. Remember what I mentioned earlier, this capsule is further divided into 2 seasonal groups: casual work—fall/winter and casual work—spring/summer. The first time I examined the color capsules in my fall/winter capsule wardrobe I discovered that I had 9 total colors—7 of these were color capsules (more than 1 garment) and 2 of these were color accents (only 1 garment) (Table 5).

Table 5: *Color and Accent Capsules Within the Occasion Capsule— Casual work*

| Occasion Capsule | | Occasion Capsule | |
| Casual work—fall/winter | | Casual work—spring/summer | |
Color Capsule	Color Accent	Color Capsule	Color Accent
Denim	Chestnut	Navy	Gray
Navy	Blush	White	Olive
Black		Black	Light Blue
Ivory		Turquoise	Tan
Tan		Denim	Blush
Gray		Ivory	Yellow
Wine		Cobalt	Purple
			Pink
			Teal

In general, my fall/winter capsule wardrobe functioned well and was pleasing to the eye. I was able to assemble outfits easily, and I felt that the wardrobe contained enough variety to keep me from feeling that I was wearing the same colors day after day.

My spring/summer capsule wardrobe was the exact opposite. This side of my closet looked a bit out of harmony. There were a lot of colors, and I often found it difficult to get dressed in the morning. This wardrobe had 16 total colors, 7 of these were color capsules and 9 of these were color accents (Table 5). Right off the bat you can see that one of my problems was that I owned more accent colors than core colors in this wardrobe. The second issue was that the accent colors did not always work well with my color capsules. The accent color might pair well with just 1 color capsule. The lack of cohesion between the color capsules and accent colors in my spring/summer wardrobe was the reason why I struggled to assemble outfits with this wardrobe capsule.

This doesn't mean that every color in a wardrobe has to pair well with every other. It's perfectly fine to own a wardrobe containing more than only 1 or 2 color accents. After all, the sporadic addition of an accent color adds interest to what would otherwise become a standard outfit. Color accents can keep your favorite outfit combinations feeling fresh and new. However, owning a *lot* of accent colors makes assembling and remixing outfits a challenge. Since my end goal is to use more of my clothes, more often, being able to remix pieces easily is one way for me to use the items frequently. This means that my accent colors need to work well with my color capsules *and* that the total number of accent colors for my wardrobe capsules is limited to a smaller number (no more than 2 or 3).

Understanding the color capsules within your wardrobe helps to explain why your wardrobe isn't working well for you. Color capsules can also serve as your guide when you are managing your occasion capsules, helping you figure out what to donate when you edit your closet, what to add when you want something new, and how to transition and evolve your wardrobe over time as your lifestyle needs change.

In this chapter you dissected your wardrobe into all of its subsequent parts, became familiar with what's inside, how much it cost you, and what capsules you need based on occasion, established a rough estimate of how often you use each one, and discovered if you have too many (or not enough) color capsules and accent colors in your wardrobe. With this information you can craft a dream closet that holds a wardrobe that you will love and feel confident in. And when you love what you have, you don't want to shop for something new. But before you can start to organize your closet, there is one thing that you must do first: get the stuff that you aren't using out of your way. And the next 2 chapters will help you do just that.

Chapter 2 recap:

*Know and understand what your closet has,
and what your closet needs.*

Hit The Brakes:
Write down everything that is in your wardrobe

- Creating a list of what's inside your closet will teach you the following about your current wardrobe including: what you own, what it cost you, and where you have too little or too much

Hit The Brakes:
Pinpoint the number of capsule wardrobes in your closet

- List all of the occasions that you participate in over 1 year so that you understand what capsules you need in your wardrobe

Hit The Brakes:
Figure out how often you need each occasion capsule in your wardrobe

- Mark how often you will use each occasion capsule in 1 year, then rank low, moderate, or high to decide roughly how large or small each capsule should be

Hit The Brakes:
Study the color capsules within your wardrobe

- Group your wardrobe into color capsules (more than 1 item of the same color is found in your closet) and color accents (only 1 item of a specific color); too many accent colors might be one of the reasons why you struggle to put together an outfit

Knowledge can lead to action. A thorough examination of what's inside your closet becomes the foundation that you will build upon to help you shape your current closet into your dream closet.

Chapter 3

Cleaning out your closet - The basics

Make space for only the good stuff

Every year when springtime rolls around, I know that I can count on 3 things: floral scents, rising temperatures, and an overabundance of advice on how to clean out my closet. Standing in line at the supermarket I'll see one magazine headline after another telling me to "Spring Clean Your Closet" and "How to Clean Out and Organize Your Closet Like a Pro." On the internet, webpages and social media sites talk about "Expert Tips for Spring Cleaning Your Closet" and "The Types of Clothes to Get Rid of Immediately." If you read more than 1 or 2 of these articles you are going to notice 2 things every one has in common: 1) the information is rarely different from one article to the next, right down to the repetitive headlines, and 2) the expert tips and advice promise that your closet will become neater, cleaner, and more organized, and will hold only the things that you love and want to wear, all because you simply took the time to do a closet edit. This optimism is nice, but what people don't always tell you is the downside to a closet edit. It's *boring!* And it can take up a lot of your spare time, often hours upon hours.

Sometimes cleaning out your closet can't even be finished in a single day, especially if you haven't done a thorough closet review in a long time.

If you are a shopaholic, or you just happen to own a large wardrobe, then the thought of editing your closet might seem overwhelming, and you would be right. It's going to be exhausting, stressful, and tedious. So why should you do it? After all, we all have too many things to do, and not enough hours in the day to do them, and I know I can think of a lot of other things that I would rather do in my free time. So why bother? Because despite the repetitive nature, all of those promises from advice columns and checklists have some tangible and emotional benefits to cleaning out your closet, including:

- **Space:** Everything will get its own "spot," better space utilization, empty areas feel "bigger," and the visual of open space often reduces stress levels and provides a sense of relief

- **Time:** Less time spent organizing and cleaning, improved ease in finding items and putting together outfits, and available time to spend on something not wardrobe related

- **Money:** Knowing what you have prevents buying repeats of what you already own and resale and consignment provides cash for something else

- **Feeling good:** Decluttering a closet provides feelings of accomplishment, empowerment, and a sense of a new beginning

Organizing and editing your closet is a lifelong process. Changes to your body size and lifestyle needs over time will have you faced with the task of cleaning out your closet time and time again. It's a boring chore that you can't escape forever, but if you know how to effectively clean out your closet you can at least make the task easier and faster to do.

Now roll up your sleeves, grab a strong cuppa tea, and let's get the basic, boring stuff out of the way so that we can work on the fun stuff later.

Hit The Brakes:
Give yourself a deadline

When you finally decide that you are going to clean out your closet, the first thing you probably want to do is to open it up, grab a few bags, and jump right in. But before you get started there's one question that I recommend that you answer first. How long do you want to do this? Choosing a start and stop time before you begin takes the pressure off of feeling like you have to finish everything in a single day, especially if you have a large and messy closet. After all, we are talking about editing a closet, not standing in the ER trying to save a life, so why stress yourself out, right? Unless you have an outside circumstance giving you a tight deadline (eg, upcoming move or remodeling), you probably don't really have to do everything all at once. You can break up the process into mini steps. My preferred way to edit my personal closet is to pick one category to review at a time. For example, set aside 1 hour to sort through 1 stack of jeans. Another day, devote 45 minutes to reviewing a small handful of tops. By dividing and conquering, the task of clearing out an unruly closet will become manageable and less intimidating. If you want a successful closet editing session you have to set the time frame and the goal before you begin.

Hit The Brakes:
Decide where your clothes are going

Now that you know how long and which category you are going to focus on during your closet editing session, you have to make one more decision. You must decide where the clothes are going to go. A favorite charity? A close friend? A family member? A homeless shelter? Sell them? Without a destination for your unwanted stuff, it's not always that easy to get rid of it all. Instead, you want to hold onto items because "there's nothing wrong with it and I might need it someday." Does this sound familiar? The problem with this line of reasoning is that you've already spent the money! And if you are not wearing something in your closet, well I have bad news for you, unworn clothing is wasted money. But, if you know that your unwanted and unused clothes are going to go to someone who will love and use them right away, that may be the little push that you need to let go of something.

My favorite option for unwanted stuff is to give it to someone that you know, usually a friend or family member. As I review what to keep or purge I think about if any of the garments in question will work for my friend. Purging with my friend in mind benefits both of us. It allows me to declutter my closet while also acting as a fashion stylist for my friend (I get to dress her up). She gets the exhilaration of receiving new-to-her clothes. Nothing feels better than when we get together for coffee, dinner, or a movie and I see her sporting my old things. The clothes that were making me unhappy get a second chance. Now they bring her joy, and that in turn is a lovely feeling for me as well. You can also donate your clothes to a local organization or charity. A few examples include: Salvation Army, Goodwill, Dress for Success, Pickup Please, shelters, or your local church.

Another option for cast-off clothing that has really helped motivate me to get rid of my stuff is to attend a clothing swap. At a clothing swap everyone brings a set number of items (usually 10 or less) and the attendees trade, with the leftover clothing donated to an agreed upon charity or organization. Once again I get to appreciate that the clothes that were unworn and unwanted by me will have a new lease on life with someone else.

In addition to donating and swapping your clothes you can try to sell your clothes at consignment stores, Ebay, Poshmark, Threadflip, Plato's Closet, etc. When you sell your clothes you get a little extra cash in your pocket, which is always nice. Some places will even allow you to sell your clothes and donate a percentage of the proceeds to charity. Another option is that you can try to repurpose your clothes. A few examples include: turn jeans into shorts, cut up tops into rags, modify a dress into a skirt or top, etc. And finally the last place you can put clothes that are not in a suitable shape to donate or repurpose is the trash bin. No matter which option you choose, when you know what you are going to do with your unwanted clothes it's often a lot easier to clean out your closet.

Hit The Brakes:
Declutter with a checklist

Alright, you've committed time to clean out your closet and your cast-offs have a destination, it's now time to begin. You are going to sort your clothing into 4 piles: keep, repair, donate, or toss. Decluttering with a checklist helps you to stay focused while also keeping you aware of the major reasons for why you don't want to use something that you own. Use these 6 questions to decide where each item goes:

1. Does it fit?

2. Does it itch, scratch?
3. Is it worn out?
4. Do I wear it?
5. Do I love it?
6. Does it project the image I want?/Does it fit my personal style?

The questions regarding fit and use are often the 2 areas where people struggle with making a decision. That is why the next 3 *Hit The Brakes* tips are going to tackle different aspects of these two areas to help you in making your decision.

Hit The Brakes:
Purge what doesn't fit your current BODY

After you have gotten rid of the easy-to-purge items, everything with obvious flaws, you'll have to start thinking longer and harder about your selections. Dressing in clothes that fit your current body is one way to raise your confidence and self-esteem, and that's why improper fit is your next target. This task is really not going to be a whole lot of fun and it's definitely the most time-consuming, but what you have to do now is critically look at the fit of your clothes. Anything that doesn't fit your current size or body shape has got to go. This means that you'll have to spend the time to try on *everything* that you own. And if you have a lot of clothes, this could take a while. Now before you roll your eyes at me, or start muttering that you think I'm crazy, I want you to consider this: if you don't even want to waste the time trying it on, why wouldn't you want to get rid of it? Surely your most loved and have to keep items deserve at least that much attention, right?

When my wardrobe was very large and I edited my closet for the first time, I spent an entire week going through my wardrobe. And occasionally I would come across something that I didn't even want to try on. Every time that happened the item in question went right into the donate pile. But what about the clothes that are in good condition, but I'm "saving" for when I lose or gain weight? Do those have to go too? Yes! Consider this: when you finally reach the goal you've set for your body, are you really going to want to start wearing the old clothes that have been hanging in your closet, or are you going to want to go out and celebrate your success by buying something that fits the new you? If you are someone who will want to buy something new, there is no point in saving clothes for a later date, because you aren't going to wear them later anyway. Remember, the purpose of this tip is to own a closet filled with clothes that you can use—*today*.

For everything you try on, carefully evaluate the fit in a mirror. Oftentimes clothes will have obvious fit issues or are just plain uncomfortable to wear. For example, you see a muffin top from trousers or jeans that are too tight in the waist or don't have the correct rise. The top that was lovely on the hanger is hugging on you in all the wrong places or gaping at the buttons on the front when you put it on. The dress looks like a paper sack because it's too large. If the garment is too big, too small, too tight, or just pinches or rubs in a way that is uncomfortable for you, there is no reason for it to take up valuable space in your wardrobe.

As you review your clothes you might stumble on something that doesn't fit, but you can't seem to let go of anyway. There are 2 times when it is perfectly OK to break the rules and keep something. The first exception is pregnancy or a medical condition, the situations when you are going to be a different size or have a specific wardrobe need for a known, relatively short length of time. And that's the key to this exception—knowing the length of time that you are unable to use most of your wardrobe. After all, I don't expect a woman who is going to be sporting maternity clothes for 9 months to toss her entire wardrobe just because she's pregnant. The same holds true, for example, for someone who broke their leg and is wearing a cast for 6 to 12 weeks. But if you don't know how long it will be until you can wear the clothes again, then it's probably time for that garment to find a new home. The second exception is anything with sentimental value. Most often these pieces are from life events: wedding, prom, first trip abroad, etc. If the item in question is irreplaceable because of the emotional value, then go ahead and keep it. You have to be really careful with sentimental possessions though—own too many and they can quickly fill up your closet with stuff that you can't use, but don't want to get rid of. You have to look long and hard at the things you decide to keep because of their sentimental value so that they don't start overcrowding your closet. Speaking of keeping things that you can't wear leads us right into the next *Hit The Brakes*.

Hit The Brakes:
Purge what doesn't fit your current LIFESTYLE

Removing the clothes that no longer fit your current body is one angle that you can use to edit your wardrobe. A complementary viewpoint is looking at what doesn't fit your current lifestyle. In Chapter 2, you recognized what wardrobe capsules you need in 1 year. These capsules were selected because of the requirements of your daily life. Shopping for stuff that doesn't fit your day-to-day life is a common trap that people run into when shopping for clothes, especially if you like to shop a lot. For a long time, I would purchase items for the future, instead of pieces that I could use today. I worked full-time in a business formal setting and attended classes at night, yet my closet was filled with sexy black dresses for "someday when I go out." While my idea of going out was me sporting revealing dresses paired with high heels, the reality was that when I went out, it was to go to work, the classroom, or the grocery store. None of those situations required a sexy black dress.

I'd find myself shopping in the stores and come across an outfit that would be perfect for a safari vacation, so I purchased it. The fact that I had no plans for going on a safari vacation didn't matter. I would stumble across a pencil skirt that actually fit me and I would add it to my wardrobe, despite the reality that in my day-to-day life, I prefer to wear jeans. My mindset was, let's forget about today. If I ended up in a business meeting in the future, I would be able to wear my new skirt, so I should purchase it when I found it. The more occasions I could think of, the more items I added to my wardrobe. So I would be prepared "just in case" one of those events actually occurred. Does buying clothes for your "future self" sound familiar?

When you buy something that does not work for your lifestyle today, what you are really doing is simply filling up your closet with "future self" clothes. Over time, the clothes you can't use daily start to take over your closet, preventing you from finding the stuff you really can use. Instead of quickly pulling out garments you can use today, you dig around the future self clothes to find what you need, which is a waste of time. And remember what I said earlier, unworn clothing is wasted money, and that includes clothes for those "I might need it moments."

So why do we still try to shop for this stuff and why is it even harder to get rid of it all?

When everything staring back at you from inside your closet is for a future you, the "you" who goes out on dates in sexy black dresses and goes trekking out on safari, you have a daily reminder of the things in your life you aren't doing. This daily reminder through your unworn clothing hanging in your closet might make you feel inadequate. When you aren't happy about yourself, and you're a shopaholic, you are going to shop to make yourself feel better. You begin running around in a shopping rut—you hate what you own, so you go shopping without a plan for something new, which of course you can't really use, so you once again hate what you own—thus you are moving around in a circle that has no end (Figure 3). Eventually your closet ends up filled with more things you *can't* use, than things you *can* use. In truth, you don't really have nothing to wear, you have nothing to wear for your daily life.

Figure 3: *The Shopping Rut*

When you are trying to streamline your closet, an easy target is to get rid of all of the clothes you can't use in your daily life. But letting go of the "future self" pieces might suggest to you that these occasions are not going to happen. If you don't own a kimono, you will not become the world traveler with interesting tales from a trip to Japan. If you don't have a dirndl, you'll have nothing to wear for Oktoberfest if you visit Germany. If your closet doesn't contain a sexy black dress, you'll never be the woman a man desires and you'll continue to live your life single and alone. Without the pencil skirt in your closet you'll never become the high-powered executive who participates in important business meetings. Removing these pieces from your closet feels like you are admitting that you'll never have these opportunities in the future. It feels like you are giving up, throwing in the towel on the potential for something to happen to you later in life. And you don't want to give up hope, so you promptly ignore the fact that you should give up this stuff, opting to keep it all anyway.

But your concerns couldn't be farther from the truth. Letting go of "future self" clothes doesn't mean that these future events may never happen. In fact, removing these pieces may actually lead to their occurrence instead. How? When the distraction of future self clothing is removed, you are able to stay focused on your day-to-day life. And what you do today will shape what will happen for you tomorrow. If your free time is spent thinking and shopping for clothes that you may need someday, then you aren't freeing up your brain power or your time to participate in the activities that will lead to you actually achieving your long-term goals.

The clothes that you own today should support the actions that you need to do so that you can accomplish your goals. If you really want to go on a safari, and working at a corporate job is going to give you the money to pay for it, then you need to own the clothes for the corporate job so that you can save and ultimately go on that safari. If you want to find a man that you'll fall in love with and marry someday, and you want that guy to love hiking in the woods, then you need to own the clothes that let you hike comfortably, so that you can join a hiking club and meet people with a shared similar interest.

By freeing up the space in your wardrobe from "future self" items, and avoiding spending your time and money shopping for pieces that you can't use today, you are able to focus your attention on completing the tasks that will allow you to achieve the goals that you desire in the future. That is why despite how difficult it is, you have to put the pieces that don't fit your daily life into the donate pile.

Hit The Brakes:
Eliminate all wardrobe orphans

You've already removed all of the items in your wardrobe that don't fit your current body or your current lifestyle, but you aren't done yet. Another review of your wardrobe that you can do if you really want to start shaping your closet into your dream closet is to get rid of all of the wardrobe orphans. Wardrobe orphans are the clothes in your closet that fit your current body, can be used in your daily life, and are in good condition, but for some mystery reason are seldom—if ever—actually worn.

You can spot the wardrobe orphans in your closet by these 4 features:

1. Store tags
2. Pairing ability
3. Outlier color or style
4. Prior use

The fastest way to spot wardrobe orphans is to look for store tags. Pieces that sit unworn for a length of time are wardrobe orphans. For myself, I give new purchases a personal 30-day return policy. If something is new and I haven't worn it in 30 days, it goes back to the store. Stuff that is sitting inside your closet that's never been worn is a sign that what you bought does not function well for your wardrobe. If you are not immediately using something that you bought, it's because you are choosing something else to wear instead. And if you are not reaching for that new fabulous item, then you didn't need it in your wardrobe.

The second feature of a wardrobe orphan takes a little more work and uses the information you gathered in Chapter 2. Pick the wardrobe capsule you want to work with and take all of those pieces out of your closet. Now you are going to put each item back into the closet if, and only if, you can answer "yes" to the following question.

Can you assemble the piece into an outfit?

Every time you create an outfit, put the entire ensemble (or the solo piece if you will use some of the outfit again) back into the closet. The leftover things that you could not assemble into an outfit are your wardrobe orphans. For example, if I was working with my fall wardrobe my outfits could look like this:

Outfit #1: Black Blazer + White Long Sleeve T-Shirt + Blue Skinny Jeans + Black Booties

Outfit #2: Olive Jacket + White Long Sleeve T-Shirt + Blue Skinny Jeans + Black Booties

Outfit #3: Black Blazer + Chambray Shirt + Blue Skinny Jeans + Black Booties

In the example above, I've added a total of 6 items back into my closet from my fall wardrobe: black blazer, white long sleeve T-shirt, blue skinny jeans, olive jacket, chambray shirt, and black booties. An extra bonus to creating outfits as you search for wardrobe orphans is the fact that you will now have an outfit combination that you already know works, for those days when you are getting ready in a hurry.

I highly encourage you to spend the time to put together outfits from the pieces in your wardrobe capsules, but sometimes you want to eliminate your stuff a little faster. Remember the color capsule analysis you did in Chapter 2? You can use this information to help you spot outliers even faster. Group your wardrobe by items of the same color. At the end of the group you will find a collection of pieces of a single color, for example, 1 yellow top, 1 red T-shirt, 1 orange sweater, these are your accent colors. If you aren't interested in wearing that accent color anymore, remove the item from your wardrobe. Another grouping you can do is by items of the same category. Once again, arranging your wardrobe in this manner will allow you to see the trends pretty fast. Among a collection of neutral blazers sits a bright pink one. Within a section of blue jeans you find one pair that is purple. In a sea of solid tops that are white, black, and navy, you discover a couple that are yellow and one that is an orange print. Grouping your wardrobe by category has a second advantage, you can pinpoint when the styles stand out. Among a dozen pairs of skinny jeans you have 2 bootcut pairs. Within the cardigans you find 2 button front crewnecks, yet the rest are hip length and open front. When your clothes are lumped by category, you can quickly find the garments that don't fit the style of the others in the group and consider whether to remove them from your wardrobe. You can continue to rearrange your wardrobe and further reduce its size by comparing what you have against your core color schemes and style preferences. If you are not familiar with these measures, don't worry, I'll cover them in detail in Chapter 5 because you must know this information before you shop for something new.

The final attribute you can use to spot your wardrobe orphans is the history of the item itself. A garment that was in heavy rotation for a given season may suddenly fall out of favor the next time the season rolls around again. Sometimes, frequent use leads to clothing fatigue. You simply grew tired of the item. Pieces that were part of a set or that represent a previous style or body shape can become wardrobe orphans later in their lives. When clothing lacks a sibling, it is typically pushed aside for something else. Your oldest clothes will always be a target during a closet purge. You have to really love that item (or it has sentimental value) for you to keep it over the long term.

Letting go of the wardrobe orphans in your closet is an essential step when trying to edit your closet, particularly if you are striving for a small, highly functional wardrobe. But discovering wardrobe orphans inside your wardrobe brings about an interesting question. How do these outlier items get inside your closet in the first place? A common reason for me was because I wanted to try something new. I wore bootcut jeans for a long time. When other styles arrived in stores (skinny, straight leg, boyfriend, etc), I tried them all. And while skinny jeans became a new favorite style of mine for the winter months for tucking into tall boots, the other styles just didn't work for me. So they sat unworn in my closet until I finally realized that I should donate them.

Hit The Brakes:
Pick 1 core color

One common piece of advice that is often mentioned for streamlining a wardrobe is to limit the wardrobe to 1 core neutral color, either for one specific wardrobe capsule or for the entire wardrobe. Simply select 1 color and keep only those clothes that pair well with your chosen color. The color that all of your clothes coordinate with is now the core color of your wardrobe. Often this core color is a neutral, typically black, brown, or gray, but can also be white, ivory, taupe, or beige. And sometimes the core color is not a neutral color at all, but a complementary color instead (typically these are the colors from a color wheel, such as red, blue, orange, green, purple, etc).

I've found this tip very helpful to reduce the size of my smallest occasion capsules. For example, currently my formal work capsule has only 1 core color—black. Black shoes, black trousers, black blazers, and all of the blouses and knitwear are prints and colors that I enjoy paired with black. When I shop for work clothes, I ignore all of the garments that I would prefer to pair with brown, gray, or navy, and I hunt for black instead. Limiting this capsule wardrobe to 1 core color immediately reduced the size of this capsule. Previously, I had work clothes that paired with black, brown, and navy, which meant that I also had to own different colored shoes for each group of colors. Having only a core of black for my formal work capsule has also helped me to prevent this wardrobe capsule from unintentionally creeping up in size over time, which will be discussed in Chapter 7. Finally, I also want to point out, if you travel often and want to bring less luggage, selecting one core color will greatly reduce the amount of shoes you will need to bring for your outfits. This is a great way to pack less stuff when traveling or when you want to own a very small and cohesive wardrobe. Keeping 1 core color in mind is also helpful when you want to maintain the size of a wardrobe capsule. I'll go into more detail about traveling and shopping with 1 core color in mind in Chapter 8.

All of the tips you've read about in this chapter helped you get rid of the obvious stuff in your closet that you don't use or can't use. If you started your closet edit with a wardrobe that was already small and functional, then you are probably done. Everything that you own you use and you find getting dressed in the morning quick and easy now. But if you discover that you are still struggling to put together something to wear every day, you have a sneaky suspicion that you still own too much stuff, or you just don't like the clothes that are left in your closet (but getting rid of anything else will leave you running around naked every day), then you still have a little more work to do with your closet. Well what are you waiting for?

Read on, because in Chapter 4 we are going to figure out what you need and start the process of customizing your wardrobe into the perfect wardrobe for you and only you.

Chapter 3 recap:

Remove the obvious to edit your closet.

Hit The Brakes:
Give yourself a deadline

• Select a time frame and a goal for your closet editing session before you begin so you will stay focused and not become overwhelmed

Hit The Brakes:
Decide where your old clothes are going

• Know to whom or where your unwanted clothing is going to give yourself a nudge when you are uncertain if you should get rid of something

Hit The Brakes:
Declutter with a checklist

• Create 4 piles for your wardrobe:

1. Keep
2. Repair
3. Donate
4. Toss

• Review each item and remove anything that can't meet all of the following criteria:

1. Does it fit?
2. Does it itch or scratch?

3. Is it worn out?
4. Do I wear it?
5. Do I love it?
6. Does it project the image I want?/Does it fit my personal style?

Hit The Brakes:
Purge what doesn't fit your current BODY

- If you can't wear it with the body shape and weight you have today, then you don't need it. Exceptions to this rule include when you know how long you will not be able to wear your clothes (eg, pregnancy, medical injury, etc) and irreplaceable, sentimental items

Hit The Brakes:
Purge what doesn't fit your current LIFESTYLE

- If it is for your future self, or your fantasy lifestyle, and not your daily lifestyle, then it's time to move that piece on to a new home

Hit The Brakes:
Eliminate all wardrobe orphans

- You can spot a wardrobe orphan to donate from your closet by any of the following features:
1. Store tags
2. Can't be paired with something else you own to create an outfit

3. Is the only one of a specific color or style
4. Was once a favorite but has fallen out of favor

Hit The Brakes:
Pick 1 core color

• Select 1 core color and keep only the clothes that pair well with your chosen color to reduce the size of a specific wardrobe capsule or your entire wardrobe

Organizing and editing your closet is a lifelong process. Checklists and self-evaluation tools help you to remove the obvious items first. After you get rid of the stuff you aren't using, you then need to do a little more work to zero in on how much you need so that you will own a wardrobe that you will be happy with.

Chapter 4

Fine-tuning your closet after decluttering

Figure out how much your wardrobe needs

Have you ever cleaned out your closet and still walked away hating your wardrobe? Have you ever purged your closet, then immediately ran out and added the same amount of stuff back in? Have you ever put everything you didn't like into the donate bag, then reached in a few days later and hung everything back up, even though you really don't like it? This is all really frustrating, isn't it? Well you are not alone because it's happened to me too. I used to read one article after another on how to properly edit and organize my closet, do every single thing that the authors asked for, and end up miserable afterwards. I would successfully purge my closet then promptly add everything back, either from buying something new or raiding the donation bag. It didn't make any sense. Everyone was promising me that I would own a wardrobe that I loved and wore all of the time, yet I was always left with a wardrobe that functioned no better after my closet edits than before them. How could I make my smaller wardrobe stick over the long term? And why was my closet still not working for me anyway?

Let's focus on the closet checklists and advice first. Why don't they always work? The answer may surprise you. Most of the advice on how to clean out your closet focuses on only one form of decision making—subjective. Subjective decisions are biased opinions; in other words, what do you think about your clothes? Do you love them? Do you hate them? Will you use them? No matter how you phrase the question, the answer has to come from you. The advice on closet cleaning that you find on news media, blogs, magazine articles, commentaries, etc is repetitive because they are usually written based on the writers' opinions. Their opinions were formed into a question, and you have to use your opinion to provide the answer.

Thankfully there is another form of decision making that you can use—objective. And that's why you have me. Remember back in the Introduction when I told you that I'm not only an ex-shopaholic, but also a research scientist? Well, objective information is the foundation for scientific research. When you ask an objective question, the answer doesn't come from the individual. Your opinion no longer matters. Opinions can be based on moods, past experiences, personal values, and societal impact. Objective decisions remove all of that variability because they are based on just the facts and nothing more.

The underlying question all closet clean-out advice is trying to get you to answer is, will you use it? To help you, the basic steps to decluttering a closet have you evaluating the physical condition and function of the item and focusing on what you don't use. But none of these helpful suggestions guide you towards a critical question about your wardrobe.

What does your wardrobe need?

You can follow every *Hit The Brakes* tip in Chapter 3 and still be left with a stack of clothing that you like, looks good on you, is appropriate for the occasions of your life, and is in fine shape to continue wearing, yet you rarely get to wear it and you are struggling with whether you should really let it go. When this happens it is time to shift the focus and start reducing the overall *size* of your wardrobe. And I have a few options for how you can figure this out.

Hit The Brakes:
Apply math to identify your ideal wardrobe size

The fastest and most straightforward way to decide out how much you need in your wardrobe is to calculate it. When you use math to figure out how much clothing you should own, you take all of the emotion out of the decision. After all, the numbers are not going to lie. In order to calculate your ideal wardrobe size, you must know the answers to the following 4 questions:

1. How many days before you do laundry?
2. How many pieces are in your outfits?
3. How often do you want to repeat an outfit?
4. How long is the season you have to sport the clothes?

I'm going to walk you through the math with myself as the hypothetical example, so grab your calculator and let's start number crunching.

Question #1 and Question #2 (How many days before you do laundry and how many pieces are in your outfits?):

I do laundry every 7 days (once a week) and each outfit consists of 2 items, a top and a bottom.

Days until laundry X amount of items in outfit = total items

7 days X 2 items = 14 items

This information is a starting point. By answering questions #1 and #2, I now understand how much clothing I require for a week's worth of outfits. But for many people, including myself, 7 days of clothing is too little. I'm not going to repeat every single outfit, every single week. I want more variety. Therefore, I replaced laundry frequency with repeat desire (Question #3).

Question #3 (How often do you want to repeat an outfit?):

I want to repeat an outfit every 2 weeks.

Days until outfit repeat X amount of items in outfit = total items

14 days X 2 items = 28 items

This question has identified how much clothing I require for 2 full weeks of individual outfits. And if my wardrobe is cohesive, I'll be able to re-mix the items, allowing me to create additional outfits, while also extending the length of time until I repeat a look. At first glance the 28 items from Question #3 may not sound like a lot of clothes, and it's not. But this question is only looking at how many items of clothes you need for one season. Since I am dealing with a 4-season climate, if I only ever wear 2 items per outfit, the total for my wardrobe would be 112 items (4 x 28 = 112). Since my Business Casual capsule wardrobe is organized into 2 seasons; a fall/winter capsule wardrobe and a spring/ summer capsule wardrobe, I would divide the total by 2, giving me 56 items per capsule wardrobe.

Of course, I still have to address the issue of living in a constantly changing climate. To ensure that you have enough variety for each season, the final question takes a look at how often you will actually wear your outfits during a given season.

Question #4 (How long is the season you have to sport the clothes?):

The length of the season will affect how many times I can repeat an outfit. The number of days I want to have before I repeat an outfit (14 days from Question #3) are applied to the total length of the season that I can wear the outfit. For example, the fall season is 3 months (12 weeks or 84 days) and I want to repeat my outfit every 14 days.

Length of season / days until outfit repeat = rate of outfit repeats

84 days / 14 days = 6 repeats

By repeating my clothes every 2 weeks, and having 3 months to wear the outfits, I am only able to repeat my outfit 6 times during the season. Suddenly, repeating outfits every 2 weeks doesn't seem like a high frequency anymore does it?

Using math is very helpful in figuring out your ideal wardrobe size, but it requires a fair amount of pre-determined knowledge about your clothing preferences. The assumptions you make here will greatly affect how much clothing you require for your wardrobe. Someone who likes to layer a lot will naturally end up owning a larger wardrobe than someone who doesn't.

When I first calculated how much clothing I need in a year, I thought there was no way I can get by with only 112 items! Starting with a wardrobe that was well over 300 items I would have to purge 188 pieces, that's roughly 60% of my wardrobe, yikes! Despite the fact that I had the cold, hard numbers staring me in the face, there was no way I was going to get rid of that much of my wardrobe at one time, ever. Why can't I just do it? Easy, asking me to do a closet purge of this magnitude goes against my purging style. But before I discuss the differences in purging styles, there's something else you need to know first: wardrobe set-point.

Sometimes instead of being happy after cleaning out your, you end up walking away frustrated instead. Similar to the buzzing of a fly near the ear, something about your closet editing keeps nagging at you. This used to happen to me all of the time. No matter how thorough I was or how many items that I removed, none of my closet purging sessions would last for the long haul. I would reduce the size of my wardrobe, then daily frustrations would spur me to shop and add more. It wouldn't be too long before I would be back to a large wardrobe again. I was missing a key piece of the puzzle: what the set-point for my wardrobe was. Without this knowledge, I would remain forever unhappy and dissatisfied with my wardrobe.

The wardrobe set-point:
The number of clothes items leading to
happiness with one's wardrobe

The set-point theory is often mentioned during discussions of weight loss and obesity.[5] The set-point theory suggests that body weight is controlled through a feedback loop. The limits are genetically determined. When someone steps outside the set-point, energy and food intake are adjusted until the body falls back within

---

[5] Harris RB. Role of set-point theory in regulation of body weight. *FASEB J.* 1990;4(15):3310-3318.

range of the set-point. In the field of positive psychology, the set-point theory may be referred to as the Hedonic (or happiness) set-point. First coined in 1971 by Brickman and Campbell,[6] each person has a fixed level of happiness that our actions strive to maintain. Feelings may go above or below the set-point, but ultimately they return to fall within a pre-fixed range. An example of set-point in action is lottery winners. People who win the lottery are temporarily euphoric, but over time, this fades away and the person is no more satisfied after than before they won the lottery. In the book *The How of Happiness: A Scientific Approach to Getting the Life You Want*, by Sonja Lyubomirsky,[7] the greatest contributor to one's happiness, up to 50%, is the set-point.

For me to be able to conduct a successful closet purge I had to establish my set-point for my wardrobe. It was important for me to understand how much clothing I was comfortable owning to fit my needs as well as to satisfy my inner desire for clothing variety. When I decluttered until I owned less items than I was comfortable with (stepped below my set-point) I shopped for more. If my closet contained too many items within it (extended over my set-point), I became overwhelmed and wanted to get rid of things (Figure 4).

---

[6] Brickman P, Campbell D. Hedonic relativism and planning the good society. In Apley MH (Ed.), Adaptation-level theory: A symposium. New York: Academic Press. 1971:287-302.

[7] Lyubomirsky S. *The How of Happiness: A Scientific Approach to Getting the Life You Want.* New York: Penguin Press. 2008.

Figure 4: *The Set-Point Is An Essential Factor for Wardrobe Happiness*

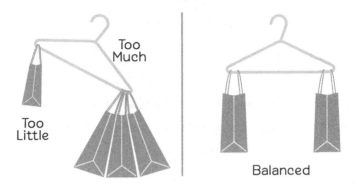

Too Much

Too Little

Balanced

The set-point for someone's wardrobe can be affected in 1 of 2 ways: big changes or small changes. The degree of change an individual's set-point will allow before it seeks to regain balance influences a person's closet decluttering style. You are either a hard-core purger or a gentle purger. A hard-core purger is someone who tackles closet purging head on. They can remove large amounts of clothing at one time, feel proud about their accomplishment, and they rarely second guess if getting rid of something was the right thing to do. A gentle purger is someone who tackles their closet purging in small doses. Attempting to purge large amounts at one time causes them to panic and go into hunter-gatherer mode, they have to run out and quickly fill in the self-perceived holes in their wardrobe.

Hard-core purger:
Comfortable with big changes to the wardrobe

versus

Gentle purger:
At ease with small changes to the wardrobe

A successful closet edit leaves you with a wardrobe that you love to own. Everything inside suits not only your current lifestyle and personal style, but you also actually wear your clothes. Using math is one way to figure out how much stuff you should own in your wardrobe. If you calculate how much you need, *your closet has a lot of clothes that you should get rid of,* and you are a hard-core purger, then you can probably stop after purging—your closet edit is now complete. However, if you are a gentle purger like me, or you simply want another option to clear out your closet that doesn't require using a calculator, one of the closet challenges coming up next may help you.

Hit The Brakes:
Participate in a closet challenge to figure out how much you need

All of the closet challenges in this section have one thing in common—they are variations on the wait and see strategy. Each one will have you figuring out what you need over a pre-specified period of time. No matter what your purging style is, sometimes when you edit your closet you run into a brick wall. You've calculated what your ideal wardrobe size should be, and don't believe the numbers. Or you've spent hours (or maybe even days) reviewing your clothes, trying them on, and using your personal knowledge to decide what to keep and what to let go of, and you still think that you have too much stuff. If you find yourself tired, overwhelmed, and you just don't want to do this anymore, you've gotten stuck. Read through the following 4 closet challenges, and select the challenge that will work best for you based on your purging style to help jump-start your closet edit.

Closet challenge #1—Hanger flipping

This challenge works best for someone who is not only a hard-core purger, but also a visual person. You'll see what you wear, as well as how much you are using (or not using) daily during the challenge time frame, then get rid of the unworn stuff at the end. That's the key factor for this method, getting rid of all of the unworn clothes.

This wardrobe challenge has 4 steps:

1. Turn all of the hangers on the closet rod so that they are facing backwards, ie, the "wrong way."
2. Select a deadline date (30 days, 3 months, 6 months, etc).
3. Rotate the hangers back to the "right way" as you wear your stuff.
4. Everything on hangers facing the "wrong way" by the deadline date is purged from your wardrobe.

If you have a large wardrobe and you are a hard-core purger, removing all the excess at the end of the challenge is easy to do. However, if you are a gentle purger like me, and you're starting out with a lot of clothes, this challenge may not be the best option. Why? In my case, the first time I tried hanger flipping my deadline date was 30 days. I flipped all of my hangers and promptly went on with my life, not giving a second thought to what I was using in my wardrobe. When the 30 days were up, I greedily returned to my closet anticipating drinking from the glass of success. Instead, I was disappointed. After 30 days it looked like I had barely worn any of my clothes. Despite the evidence staring me in the face, I balked. There was no way I was going to discard more than 80% of my wardrobe! Not one to be discouraged, I repeated the challenge, this time lengthening it to 60 days. My result was almost the same. Once again I had many articles of unworn clothing at the end of the challenge period. The thought of discarding such a large portion of my wardrobe caused me to shake like a leaf in the wind.

If you try this challenge and find yourself in a similar situation, asked to purge too many clothes items, too fast, don't worry. Challenge options that work well for editing large wardrobes at a slower pace are coming up a little later in this chapter.

Closet challenge #2—Seasonal edit

With one small tweak you can modify the hanger flipping challenge into a seasonal challenge. The difference here is that you use the end of the season, not a number of days, as your deadline date. Moving the deadline date to the end of a season provides you the opportunity to sport as many items as you can during the season. This challenge is ideal for 2 types of people—the hard-core purger with a large wardrobe to edit and the gentle purger who is looking to fine-tune their wardrobe. Because you're working with a seasonal deadline, if you can't fit in wearing the item over the length of one season, it'll be some time before the appropriate season rolls around again so that you can wear your old clothes. For example, I live in a 4-season area, with each season roughly 3 months long. For my clothes left unworn at the end of a season, it'll be 3 more seasons—that's 9 months—until I can try again. That's a long time to wait to wear something! Clearly, if I could survive without using the item over a season, I did not need to own it.

One year I tried this method for the summer season. At the end of the summer (3 months) I purged all of my summer clothes that went unworn. If you had asked me at the start of the summer season how many pairs of shorts I thought I would need, I would have answered at least 7. After all, there are 7 days in a week and the summer lasts for 3 months. Curious how many shorts I really needed? Two. That's right, only 2. How was this possible? Easy. The dress code at my current job doesn't allow me to wear shorts and I work 5 days a week. That leaves me only 2 days every week to wear my shorts. Also, on the weekends I'm usually in air conditioning and I typically run cold. With 2 pairs of shorts in my summer wardrobe I am able to sport each pair of shorts only once per week, for the entire summer season. It turns out that 2 pairs of shorts is just enough for me.

Even on a beach vacation 2 pairs of shorts is sufficient for my needs. If I rotate the 2 pairs of shorts, and the holiday lasts for 7 days, I can wear one pair of shorts 3 times and the other pair 4 times during the given week. Since I am normally only on vacation for 1 week at a time, and spend the majority of that time in beach clothing (bathing suits and cover ups), I don't wear my shorts for many hours each day. Repeating 2 shorts works just fine.

This challenge works well to help you figure out if you own too much of a particular item (such as shorts), but if you have a large wardrobe, and you're a gentle purger like me, you'll need to keep in mind one thing. For myself, when I first tried this challenge I had a large wardrobe that I needed to edit. I noticed that as I was moving through the seasons I was leaving a lot of clothes unworn. This caused me to panic. I stopped selecting my "favorite" items and I started focusing on "rescuing" my clothes from the dreaded end-of-the-season purge. I didn't want to donate bags and bags of clothes anymore. This meant instead of repeating items often, I tried to create new outfits daily, so that I could wear as many pieces as possible throughout the season. This shift in behavior was defeating the purpose of this challenge. The daily visual of lots of unworn clothing was not helping me, it was serving as a trigger instead. I had to eliminate the visual reminders of what I was not using by completing a different challenge.

Closet challenge #3—Purge as you go

If you are someone who doesn't like visual reminders of the stuff that you aren't using, and you are a gentle purger, then this might be the challenge for you. You only have 2 steps to do here: 1) set a length of time for your challenge and 2) get rid of your clothes as you go. If you pull something out of your closet to wear and you find yourself putting it back because you really don't want to, change course and put the piece in the donate bag instead. This challenge is really that simple, you use it or lose it. After all, let's face the facts here, if you don't want to wear it today, why would you suddenly want to wear it tomorrow? For this challenge to be successful you will need to keep 2 things in mind: 1) you don't second guess your decision to remove something from your wardrobe and 2) you don't try to rescue stuff from the donate bin if it sits around your home for a while.

Closet challenge #4—Wear everything twice

This challenge is especially helpful when you have already gotten the size of your wardrobe pretty small, and you just want to tweak it a bit. Your task is simple: select one of your wardrobe capsules from Chapter 2 and get rid of everything that you don't wear twice in 1 month. Sporting an item only twice within 1 month isn't that often, and it allows for plenty of variety. For example, if you own 15 pairs of jeans, it would take slightly over 2 weeks before you have to start repeating them. In 1 month, you can use all of your jeans twice. Owning a total of 15 jeans doesn't appear to be as bad now, if you don't mind only wearing them twice in a month. But remember all those sweaters I counted back in Chapter 2? When you start doing the math, if the month has 30 days and I want to wear each one twice, I'm only going to be able to wear 15 of them. I can reduce the size of my sweater collection by half and still have enough variety to wear each one only twice.

Of course, as a gentle purger I'm not going to feel comfortable removing half of my sweater collection at one time. The thought of giving away huge chunks of my wardrobe causes me to break out in a cold sweat, I completely panic! Does this sound familiar? But no one ever said that when you edit your closet, you had to get rid of everything right away. You can go slow instead.

Hit The Brakes:
When you're undecided on whether
to let something go, pressure test it

This is a great exercise for someone who needs a little extra time to feel comfortable with letting go of their clothes. To test if your decision was the correct decision, follow these 3 steps:

Step #1: Store questionable items in cardboard boxes or opaque shopping bags, thus placing them on "hold."

Step #2: Revisit that box after a set amount of time.

Step #3: Donate/Discard the unused items.

The reasoning here is 2-fold: 1) if you haven't thought about the item after a specific length of time, then you will not notice that the item is now gone; and 2) if you haven't opened the box even once during the time frame, you don't need what's inside the box. Decluttering with the box method prevents purging guilt. The clothes are not removed from the home, just the closet itself. This provides ample time for you to reconsider your decision. Then, when the deadline date arrives, the results are instantaneous. The clothes are already packed up and ready to go.

I've used every *Hit The Brakes* tip I've mentioned so far to clean out my closet and still ended up frustrated with my wardrobe. How is that possible? Easy. Despite all of the great advice on how to edit my closet I never knew when to stop or keep going during my closet editing sessions. I'm also a gentle purger, and would struggle to remove lots of clothes from my home at one time, yet I'd feel guilty at how little of my wardrobe I was using. I wanted a smaller wardrobe, but after I cleaned out my closet I would fail to maintain the size of my wardrobe in the long term. This uncertainty and embarrassment with myself caused me to continuously step outside the range of my set-point for my wardrobe, stalling my closet decluttering and sparking my desire to shop. And I had yet another problem. Despite my best efforts, I was still selecting the wrong clothing to keep. If any of this sounds like you, then you need a closet challenge that takes into account all of the variables affecting your wardrobe:

- How many capsules you own and what size they need to be

- How much clothing you wear regularly

- How much you do or don't like to repeat your outfits

- How fast you can let go of the clothes that you don't wear

- How to gradually lower your wardrobe set-point

Hit The Brakes:
Use The DH Closet Challenge
to manage your wardrobe

The Darling Husband (DH) Closet Challenge was devised by my DH, who was tired of watching me struggle with managing the size of my wardrobe. At the time I had already completed 3 years of researching and trying various challenges to reduce the size of my wardrobe. Similar to someone on a diet, every tip would work for a little while. But ultimately it would fail to help me maintain a smaller wardrobe over the long term.

The DH Closet Challenge is a threshold experiment. As one of the most basic measurements of perception, a threshold is the point or level at which something changes. The primary question of a threshold experiment is, "How far can I go before I react?" Threshold experiments are common in the field of psychophysics. Researchers in this field use stimuli that can be objectively measured, thus providing information about the relationship between physical stimuli and sensation (or response). Thresholds can affect everything that a person does because humans are always using their 5 senses (touch, taste, smell, hearing, and vision). An example of a threshold experiment uses the sense of vision; "How far away can one detect the flame of a candle?" or "How far away can a car be before one detects the headlights?"

In the case of The DH Closet Challenge, the question is applied to one's wardrobe. "How long can I go before I need a change?" The goal of this challenge is simple. Add as few items of clothing as possible, then see how long you can last until the desire for more has grown too strong to ignore. In doing so, you can pin-point the number of clothes items you need and how often you are comfortable with repeating these items during a given season. With this knowledge, you'll know how much clothing you actually use and you'll have a benchmark number for closet edits/purges/ additions in the future. You'll also figure out what things you like most, because anything you like you're going to want to wear.

Determining the amount of clothes that I need, over a long period of time, allowed me to identify how much clothing I wear on a regular basis, while also providing myself enough time to adjust to the smaller number of clothes in my wardrobe. And since I didn't purge anything at the start of the challenge, I didn't panic. There were no holes to fill because all of my clothes were just relocated for a little while.

Rules for The DH Closet Challenge

4 Steps To Begin:

1. **Decide on a start date.** For me, that was November 1, 2013.
2. **Remove all items out of the working closet.** The working closet will be the space I visit daily to create an outfit.
3. **Put all other items into a "boutique."** This may be called the hidden holding zone or wardrobe benchwarmers. The purpose of the "boutique" is to house all of the clothes that I can "shop" for when I desire a "new" addition to my working closet. These pieces are fair game to be purged or used at a later date. Originally I had my "boutique" in a separate

closet. Unfortunately, this location was short lived. The excessive number of clothes combined with the heavy weight of the items stacked tightly together, caused a hurricane in the closet. The closet rod broke and shelving broke and everything ended up on the floor. This forced me to move the "boutique" back into my working closet. I stored everything for the "boutique" in opaque shopping bags with post it notes on the outside indicating the category and season for the items. The tops of the bags were covered with tissue paper. The point of the "boutique" is to keep the items out of sight, out of mind, yet still accessible.

4. **Add in items to the working closet as you wear them.** Suggestions for shopping the "boutique" are covered after the *Ground Rules*. Additionally, the tips on how to shop a retail store covered in Chapter 6 can also be applied to shopping the boutique.

Ground Rules:

1. **Add in enough clothes from the boutique to get to the first laundry cycle.** I do laundry once a week, so that meant I was only selecting outfits for the first week, a total of 7 outfits. When selecting outfits, I had to keep in mind to wear clothing items as often as possible before I would feel the need to wash them.

2. **Shop the "boutique" for "new" items.** Continue to add items to increase the wardrobe size of the

working closet, without adding in entirely new full outfits. Since I do laundry every week, by the end of week 2 I had 14 outfits, with multiple pieces from week 1 repeated to create the outfits for week 2. Decide how many times you can wear an item before you're bored with it. Have I sported a top 3 weeks in a row and I'm now already bored with it? Am I comfortable wearing the same blazer 3 times in 1 week? Do I need 14 individual outfits before I am ready to start the repeat cycle again? Items that were pulled from the "boutique" *and* worn, cannot be returned. If I no longer want to wear the item, it must be purged, consigned, or donated. I'm not comfortable returning worn items to a store, so I should not return worn items to the "boutique" either.

3. **Maintain a one in/one out policy for new additions.** The ideal scenario during the challenge is that you don't shop for anything new the entire time. As your clothes wear out, you shop the boutique instead. But the chances of actually doing that might be rather low, especially if you are a shopaholic like I was when I started the challenge. Or you may not have anything in the boutique that can replace your worn-out clothes. Regardless of the reason, any time you want to add something new to your wardrobe you have to enforce the one in/one out policy. The one in/one out policy

maintains the size of a wardrobe over time, by adding and removing clothes in equal numbers.

One in/one out policy:
For every new item you add,
you must remove something old.

Here are 3 examples of using the one in/one out policy during the challenge:

Example #1: You want to add something from the boutique to your working closet. In order to do so, you'll have to donate or discard an item from the working closet. This will decrease the size of the boutique over time.

Example #2: You bought something from a retailer and you don't want to remove anything from your working closet. You can add the new purchase to the boutique if, and only if, you donate or discard an item from the boutique. This will maintain the size of the boutique over time.

Example #3: You bought something new and you one in/one out the new garment for something in the working closet. You'll have to donate, consign, or discard an item from the boutique too. This will decrease the size of the boutique over time.

While everyone's set-point for their wardrobe will be different, remember that the goals of The DH Closet Challenge are to pin-point the number of clothes items that you need and how often you are comfortable repeating items during a given season. This means that you want to keep as few clothes items as possible in your working closet and you want to wear them as much as possible. A good benchmark is to begin the one in/one out policy after you have 14 outfits. At this point you have 2 options moving forward:

Option #1—Add another new boutique outfit. With 2 weeks' worth of clothing to wear, if you want to add in yet another new outfit, then there is 1 outfit that will have to sit unworn during the next 2-week period. The key question is, are you really comfortable with letting something sit unworn for 2 weeks? If you answer yes, then go ahead and add the new outfit as you are not yet at your set-point, but now you have to wear all 13 outfits before you can consider adding another new outfit to the mix. You repeat the cycle of wearing all of your outfits before adding a new one, until you no longer want to add a new outfit anymore. Once you answer no, you have reached your wardrobe set-point and can start one in/one out with what you have in your working closet.

Option #2—Add another new boutique item. Depending on your geographic area, changing weather patterns may leave you needing a warmer or cooler weather item that's not already in your working closet. If you are missing enough warm or cool weather pieces to sport the necessary number of outfits that you need until your next laundry day, go ahead and add the additional item, as you are not yet at your set-point. If you have enough clothes for the weather, but you are just bored and want something new, you are already at your wardrobe set-point, therefore you should begin to one in/one out your new additions.

The challenge is over when there is nothing left in the boutique. To eliminate the boutique over time you have 2 options: 1) donate or discard clothes from the boutique at any time or 2) wait until you are able to one in/one out everything from the boutique into the working closet.

4 questions to ask before shopping the "boutique":

1. Can I build a new outfit combination from items I already own? Sometimes a simple swap of a top with a different bottom is all that's needed to freshen up pieces. This helped me keep the number of layering tops (long-sleeve T-shirts, light-weight knitwear) very low. I would repeat the same knit tops every week, sometimes layered underneath a blazer and other times layered with a scarf over it.

2. What can I add to stretch the use of an item? This question brought with it a few additional considerations to figure out what to add Would adding a thermal underlayer let a top or dress stretch into cooler weather? Can I add a blazer, cardigan, or sweater over a top for more warmth? Would a button-down shirt underneath a summer dress work for fall? In general, adding layering pieces really helped me stretch summer items into fall and fall items into winter months.

3. What item am I trying to create an outfit with? To prevent blindly grabbing items from the "boutique," I had to first decide what piece I wanted to build a new outfit around. The working closet item that was worn the least was always my starting point. If I wasn't wearing it regularly, I either needed something to "make it work" as Tim Gunn says, or it's time to purge the item.

4. Am I a day behind on laundry? How often I do laundry will heavily influence how many outfits I need. If I fall behind more than a day or2, I'm going to want (or need) to start pulling for new pieces. But if I typically do laundry once a week on the same day, I've inflated how much I need. Only add something to the working closet when you really don't have anything to wear because your entire wardrobe is in the laundry bin.

Insights From The DH Closet Challenge

The DH Closet Challenge was an eye-opening experience for me. For the first time I was able to see how much clothing I was (and was not) wearing in a given season as well as what clothes I really loved to wear. Curious what I discovered? Good, because I'm going to walk you through my findings.

I lived in a 4-season climate when I started the challenge in November 2013, which was halfway through our fall season. At the end of our fall/winter season I had only 54 items! With only 54 items used for the fall/winter, I was left with 134 items in the "boutique." This is a list of the 54 items I ended the fall/winter season with:
  • 6 bottoms (jeans and trousers)

- 2 hoodies

- 12 toppers (this includes pullover sweaters, blazers, and cardigans)

- 7 knits (used for layering)

- 4 gear items (2 toppers [fleece, hoodie], 1 layering knit [turtleneck], and 1 bottom [jean])

- 1 shirt (for layering)

- 3 long-sleeve T-shirts (for layering)

- 4 tanks (for layering)

- 6 thermals (for layering)

- 5 scarves

- 2 workout outfits (2 tops and 2 bottoms)

When did I reach my wardrobe total for fall/winter?

I reached my final total of 54 items, during week 7 of the challenge. That was a lot earlier than I anticipated, less than 2 months! I did not stray very far from this number (weeks 9 and 12 I had 55 items) for the remaining weeks.

Out of the final total, 26 items were utilitarian in their function and were for specific activities or as a layering item. These included: gear items (4), workout outfits (2 outfits, 4 items), thermals (6), tanks (4), long-sleeve T-shirts (3), and scarves (5).

That left me with only 28 items for outfit remixing (bottoms [6], hoodies [2], toppers [12], knits [7], shirt [1]). I left the shirt and knits (which were used for layering) as part of the pieces for outfit remixing, as these items were worn without a topper (blazers, cardigans, jackets, or sweaters) on rare occasions.

Items worn the most were still only worn 12 times during the fall/winter season. Since I remember some items being workhorses and worn often, this means items were either worn once a week, almost every week, or worn often within the same week, to be left unworn on subsequent weeks.

How often did I overhaul my working wardrobe?

My first purge of working closet items was during week 5 (2 items), because these pieces wore out. I also purged again during week 9 (4 items) and week 12 (7 items). The second purge was because I had received Christmas gifts that I didn't want to store in the boutique. The third purge at week 12 was due to the fact that I had sorted through the boutique and assembled a few bags of clothes to donate. At the same time, I decided to update my working closet with "new" stuff from the boutique. These 3 purges result in a total of 13 items removed from the working closet during the fall/winter season for a turnover rate of 24%.

Did I shop during the fall/winter season?

Unfortunately, yes, I did shop in the retail stores and not only the "boutique" during the fall/winter season. Some of these new pieces were swapped into the working closet right away. Other items that went unworn were able to be returned. Yet 10 items I held on to, thinking

I would get around to swapping them into the working closet at some point during the fall/winter season. But I was wrong, that never happened. I finished the fall/winter season with these new additions left unworn, no longer able to be returned, and having increased the total number of items in the "boutique" because I didn't adhere to the rules and one in/one out when I added something new to my wardrobe.

What did The DH Closet Challenge tell me about my future wardrobe?

I finished the fall/winter season with 54 items. Before I continued the challenge into the spring/summer season I hypothesized what I thought the size of my wardrobe would be at the end of the challenge. If I also completed the spring/summer season with 54 items, the same number that I had for the fall/winter season, I'd only have a total of 108 items in my working closet after a year of participating in the challenge. The "boutique" would still be in business and have 80 items. And the entire size of my wardrobe, adding both working closet and boutique items would be 188 items! Since I only purged 24% of my clothes (13 items) during the fall/winter season, it would take me a long time (~6 times) to clear out a boutique holding 80 items, if I didn't do a large purge of "boutique" items. The long and short of all of these calculations was: I would still own more than I needed.

And I was shocked to discover the low number of clothes that I required for a given season. I finished the winter season with only 5 heavy-weight sweaters, 2 mid-weight sweaters, 3 blazers, 1 jacket, and 1 cardigan. That's only 12 toppers, even though we had an extremely cold winter that year. Yet the total number of sweaters in my wardrobe (when I counted both the working closet and boutique numbers) was 12, just for sweaters! Finally, none of my sweaters from the past season were in need of replacement. My "boutique" contained enough clothes to overhaul my sweater wardrobe, and I didn't even need to.

Excited by my insights from the fall/winter season, I proceeded to continue the challenge during the spring/summer season. The amount of stuff I had in my spring/summer wardrobe was almost the same number that I had in my fall/winter wardrobe—53 items:

- 8 bottoms (jeans, trousers, and shorts)

- 1 hoodie

- 10 toppers (this includes: pullover sweaters, blazers, and cardigans)

- 4 knits (three-quarter sleeve or long-sleeve T-shirt for layering)

- 5 gear items (2 jeans, 2 hoodies, 1 T-shirt)

- 3 shirts/blouses

- 10 short-sleeve T-shirts/tops

- 3 tanks

- 3 scarves

- 2 workout gear (top and bottom)

- 4 dresses

Combining the spring/summer and fall/winter totals, my working wardrobe after 1 year contained 107 items, which was very close to my hypothesis at the end of the fall/winter season that I would finish 1 year owning 108 items in the working closet. I began the challenge with almost 200 items in my wardrobe. Apparently I owned almost double the amount of clothing that I really needed.

Over the course of 1 year of The DH Closet Challenge, I learned to work with a smaller wardrobe, I honed my shopping skills, and I reduced the number of unused or rarely used clothes within my wardrobe. These were my favorite 10 take-aways that I've assembled from working with a smaller wardrobe:

1. **My ideal wardrobe size is smaller than I thought**. By week 3 I realized that I owned over 12 pairs of bottoms, yet I was content with sporting the same 5 pairs again and again. And when I added a sixth bottom to my fall/winter wardrobe, I felt overwhelmed. That extra pair of jeans put me over the threshold of jeans I preferred within my wardrobe.

2. **Poor planning leads to poor purchase decisions.** Too often I have shopped out of boredom, frustration, sadness, or some other reason that was driven by emotion and not pure need. I purged many items during the year of the challenge and the

majority of these pieces were purchases that were made without having a plan set in place before I shopped.

3. **I prefer brown (vs black) as my core neutral.** To prevent from shopping out of boredom I participated in a few wardrobe challenges. These challenges are discussed in Chapter 10. During these challenges I realized that I prefer brown as my core neutral. The brown is softer for my coloring.

4. **Clothes don't always wear out as fast as I think.** I don't mind owning duplicates of an item, but when I purchase a duplicate as a replacement piece, the item tends to sit unworn for a long time.

5. **Quality (or lack of) stands out with less clothes.** I don't think one has to purchase budget-busting clothes, but, with less clothes, quality really does stand out. This is very helpful to use as a guide for how much to spend on a purchase. If I think the item is better quality and I know I will sport the piece often, I'm more inclined to spend more. And when I want to try out something new but am not concerned with longevity, I'm comfortable spending less and knowing the item will not last long in my wardrobe.

6. **Souvenirs are impulse purchases.** Souvenirs run the risk of being wardrobe orphans just as easily as other items. Except these are even harder to purge from my wardrobe, because these pieces

are also sentimental. I had more than one souvenir item (vacations, concerts, etc) in the boutique after a year. The effect that souvenirs have on your wardrobe is coming up in Chapter 8.

7. **Pause to help prevent purchasing mistakes.** Taking time to think about my new purchases before I take off the tags gives the purchase high a chance to wear off. And I may end up returning the clothes once I am able to view them with a more critical eye.

8. **Wardrobe favorites stand out regardless of wardrobe size.** It didn't matter if I had 13 or 300 items to pick from, time and again I would grab my favorite items and repeat wearing them. The same holds true for favorite outfit combinations. Once I decide on a combination I enjoy, I tend to repeat it again and again. And this helps make getting ready in the morning really fast too.

9. **Sales are a big trigger.** The word "sale" acts like a trigger for me to shop. But an item is only a good deal if I really needed it. If it's just going to sit unworn like many other pieces in my wardrobe, then it wasn't a bargain after all.

10. **I shop less the more I like my wardrobe.** One day after completing the challenge, DH was looking for a new winter coat. He had to drag me to the mall. **ME**, *not wanting to go to a mall?!* I lamented in the car. "How did this happen?" I told him that his challenge broke me, I no longer enjoyed going

to the mall to shop. His response, "No, look at the progress you've made. Now you only shop when you need something."

Ultimately it took me 13½ months to shut down the boutique and complete The DH Closet Challenge. This challenge was a great exercise to help me recognize how much clothing I needed, desired, and used, over a long time frame. It helped me adjust to owning less clothes over time while giving me the opportunity to gradually purge what I wasn't using. I also gained insight into my personal style preferences.

Figuring out how much stuff you need is a crucial component of owning a closet that makes you happy. When you own what you need and see yourself using it all, you know that the money you've spent on your stuff was a smart decision. Another important component to loving your closet is that the stuff inside is everything that you like. Understanding what you like, the focus of the next chapter, will help streamline your shopping routine, and ensure that your clothing purchases are aligned with your wardrobe desires.

Chapter 4 recap:

Understand what you need inside your wardrobe.

Hit The Brakes:
Apply math to identify your ideal wardrobe size

- Calculate how much clothes you should own in 3 easy steps:
  1. Days until laundry X amount of items in outfit = total items
  2. Days until outfit repeat X amount of items in outfit = total items
  3. Length of seasons / days until outfit repeat = rate of outfit repeats

Hit The Brakes:
Participate in a closet challenge to figure out how much you need

- When you get stuck editing your closet, one of the 4 closet challenges will get you moving again:
  1. **Hanger flipping:** Purge everything still on a backwards facing hanger by the deadline date
  2. **Seasonal edit:** Remove everything left unworn at the end of the season
  3. **Purge as you go:** When you reach for an item and decide you don't really want to wear it, put it in the donate pile instead of back in your closet

4. **Wear everything twice:** Pick a wardrobe capsule and purge everything you don't wear twice in 1 month

Hit The Brakes:
When you're undecided on whether to let something go, pressure test it

- If you aren't ready to let go of something right away, box it up and when the deadline date rolls around, let it go

Hit The Brakes:
Use The DH Closet Challenge to manage your wardrobe

- Put your entire wardrobe in a holding zone or "boutique"

- Add in enough clothes from the boutique to get to the first laundry cycle, then continue to add items to increase the size of the working closet, without adding in entirely new full outfits

- Any time you want to add something new to your wardrobe enforce the one in/one out policy by adding and removing clothes in equal numbers

- The challenge is over when the boutique is empty, either from donating, consigning, discarding, or one in/one out the clothes

A wardrobe that functions well has all of the stuff that you need and none of the things that you don't. Once you know how much you need, maintaining, updating, and transitioning your wardrobe will be easier to do.

Chapter 5

Figuring out your personal style

Know what you like before you shop

Have you ever walked into a store knowing that you wanted to buy something, but you can't figure out exactly *what* to buy? Me too! The more choices the store has, the more overwhelmed I become. Looking around at all of the options before me I freeze, just like a deer in headlights. What do I purchase? How much should I spend? How many do I buy? Should I really get it? Do I actually need it? Is this the right style for me? Is it the right color for me? When you go shopping for something new, there are a lot of questions to ask yourself, and I never knew any of the answers.

In an attempt to bring order and purpose to my shopping trips, I looked for advice. The most common thing I ran into was top 10 lists, so I eagerly memorized them. Armed with a list of items that I "had to own"—a button-down white shirt, a little black dress, a pair of black pumps, a trench coat, etc—I prowled the retailers seeking to fill my self-imposed wardrobe holes. Reading an article about minimalism would send me off in search of items with lots of black and gray, paired with straight cuts and lines. Learning about a "Parisian wardrobe" had me looking for ballet flats, striped t-shirts, and skinny leg trousers. Reviewing a "spring trend list" would spur me to want to add pastel colors and floral prints to my currently print-free and neutral-toned wardrobe. Every time I read about a new style, or learned about trends for the upcoming season, I wanted to assemble the look for myself. I would always think, "if I just had a [Parisian, minimal, spring trend, etc] wardrobe, shopping and getting dressed would be so much easier." And each time I would end up dissatisfied. Why wasn't all of my research working for me? Because the one thing I was forgetting to acknowledge, was me!

You can read all of the advice in the world about what you should own to achieve a specific look or to keep on top of the latest trends and styles and still be stuck. Why? If these suggestions are not in line with what you want your style to be, you are going to keep running around in circles, just like I did. Which brings up a very important question that will greatly impact your wardrobe:

What's your personal style?

For a long time I couldn't answer this question. Can you? If you can't then you'll have to do a little research to hone in on what your personal style is. When you understand what you like to wear, shopping for and creating outfits from your wardrobe should become a whole lot easier for you to do.

Hit The Brakes:
Identify your personal style

Personal style is the look that you like to wear most. Your personal style consists of 5 parts: fashion style, dressing preference, signature color, body type, and lifestyle.

When your outfit covers all 5 areas of your personal style, you sport an outfit thinking "I love it." When your outfit doesn't hit all of these areas, those are the days when what you wear has you thinking "this really doesn't feel like me."

Now that you know what factors make up your personal style, let's take a look at each of these one-by-one.

Personal Style Factor #1—Fashion Style

The most talked about factor of personal style is fashion style, and while these terms are often used interchangeably they are not the same thing. Personal style is the relationship you have with your clothes and is made up of the 5 parts that I mentioned earlier. Fashion style is only one part of personal style, it refers to the distinctive manner of dress that you are attracted to. Just as there are more than 1 or 2 types of people in the world, there are more than 1 or 2 types of fashion styles, it would be impossible to list them all. The most common 8 fashion styles discussed today include: bohemian, classic, romantic, minimalist, preppy, sporty, retro, and trendsetter (Table 6).

Table 6: *Common Fashion Styles*

Fashion style	Key attributes
Bohemian	Long and loose, relaxed, individualized touches
Classic	Timeless, flattering, tailored
Romantic	Soft colors, feminine details, fabrics with drape
Minimalist	Neutrals, metallic, structured, crisp, simple
Preppy	Simple, conservative
Sporty	Practical, activity oriented
Retro	Vintage inspired, imitate previous era
Trendsetter	Creative, unique, runway inspired

Another difference between personal style and fashion style is time itself. Fashion style has an expiration date, while personal style does not. Fashion is meant to be a guide, to help you decide how you want to express yourself, thus helping you to establish your personal style.

Remember in the beginning of this chapter when I mentioned how I fervently chased every wardrobe and style must-have list I could find, but kept struggling with my wardrobe? That's because I didn't know how I wanted to express myself. I struggled to identify both my personal style and my fashion style. This indecision drove me to try lots of fashion styles, hoping that along the way I would somehow stumble upon my personal style and finally feel like "me." But I kept running into a roadblock because fashion style is only one piece of the pie for preferred style.

Before you can define your fashion style there is one thing you have to do first—create a vision board. A vision board is a collection of images that represent what you want for a specific topic, in this case, your personal style. To create a vision board you can collect images using an app such as Pinterest, clip them out of a magazine, or simply save pictures from the web onto your computer. No matter how you collect your photos, what you want to do is gather up a dozen or more pictures of outfits that you like. My favorite outfits are collected from celebrity street-style photos, blogger outfit photos, and outfit capsules by season from both magazines and store retailer web pages.

To define your fashion style, take a look at your vision board for the common themes. This is the list of themes and attributes you are looking for:

- **Colors**

Are the colors neutrals, bold, bright, dark, pastels, soft, or jewel tones?

Are the color tones warm, cool, or both?

- **Clothes**

What type of garments do you see (dresses, skirts, blazers, jackets, sweaters, cardigans, blouses, shirts, jeans, or trousers)?

Are the garment shapes loose materials and look soft to the touch or crisp and stiff with defined structure?

What details do the garments have (ruffles and bows, A-lines, crisp and tailored, etc)?

• **Outfit combination**

Is the complexity of the outfit simple (1 or 2 pieces with few or no accessories) or elaborate (heavily layered and accessorized)?

• **Outfit function**

What wardrobe capsule is this outfit for? (Casual setting, formal setting, vacation etc; if you need a refresh, wardrobe capsules were discussed in Chapter 2)

Once you've identified the key attributes from each theme, match up your result with a pre-determined fashion style. You can select one of the 8 listed in Table 6 or pick from a list on the internet. If you find that you are not fitting into a listed category, you can select the common themes among the outfits you picked and create your own.

Let's take a look at a couple of examples. If your vision board is filled with soft-toned neutrals and pastels, outfits with ruffles and bows, small prints, and soft lines and lots of dresses and skirts, then your fashion style is probably romantic. Someone with minimalist fashion style will have a vision board with neutral colors (usually black and white), crisp fabrics, structured outfits, and very few components to each outfit. When the board has earthly colors, soft fabrics, layered outfits, and is typically paired with accessories with multiple details, the fashion style is most likely bohemian. If your fashion style does not pair up with one of the pre-determined fashion styles, or if your vision board looks like it is bouncing around all over the place and has no dominant fashion style at all, simply write down the common features that you see and you will have the attributes of your fashion style. For example, if all of the outfits have layers, what are they layered with? Jackets, cardigans, or blazers? Do any of these toppers have details or are they all plain? If the outfits all have boots, are the boots flats, heeled, or wedges? Do the boots lace up, zipper, or slip on? Do the boots end at the ankle, mid-calf, knee, or mid-thigh? Are all of the outfits black and white or do they feature jewel tones? Every vision board will have some type of theme, you just have to spot what it is.

If you don't want to do a vision board, you have another option for defining your fashion style. The internet is filled with multiple-choice quizzes on this specific topic. They are often labeled as personal style quizzes, although the answer you typically get is really your fashion style. Too many quizzes exist for me to list them all, however, I've noticed that these quizzes often repeat themselves, allowing me to group the topics into 5 specific categories.

1. Favorite colors to wear (neutrals, bold, bright, dark)
2. Your ideal shoe (flats, pumps, sneakers, boots, nothing)

3. What your most comfortable outfit is (jeans and sneakers, a dress and pumps, workout gear)
4. The clothing details you are drawn to (ruffles and bows, A-lines, crisp and tailored, anything on the runway)
5. What occasion or room décor you prefer (browsing a bookstore, on a beach, park with the kids, etc, or a modern room, traditional room, Victorian room, etc)

When your fashion style falls into 1 of the 8 common fashion styles, quizzes are a great way to identify which fashion style is right for you. However, if you take a quiz and struggle with answering the questions, then your fashion style is probably not 1 of the 8 common fashion styles. If this happens, simply use a vision board to define your personal fashion style.

Vision boards and personal style quizzes can help you figure out your fashion style, but there are a few things that you need to keep in mind when using either of these tools. These tools will help to label your fashion style for a particular day, but remember that fashion itself comes with an expiration date, and vision boards and quizzes don't help you establish what your fashion style is over the long term. As time changes and your preferences and lifestyle needs change, your fashion style will also change. After all, what you like today is not necessarily what you liked 10 years ago, or what you will like tomorrow.

Secondly, when you work with a vision board or personal style quiz, you must keep in mind that sometimes there is a disconnection between what a person "likes" versus what a person "likes on themselves." I might adore the look of a Victorian room and pastel colors, but a romantic style with lots of ruffles and pastel colors does not work well on my body type or my personal coloring. I really appreciate an outfit possessing crisp lines from a tailored shirt or a pencil skirt, paired with only black and white. Yet brown and blue are far more flattering colors for me, while knit tops and jeans are less fussy to me and the pieces I enjoy sporting daily. When you are putting together your vision board you need to keep in mind if the looks you pick will fit in with the other factors of your personal style, which will be covered later in this chapter.

Another thing to keep in mind, particularly with vision boards, is the occasion capsules you identified in Chapter 2. If the outfits you picked don't fit into the capsules that you have in your wardrobe, then you need to look at what attributes of that style you can cross over into your current lifestyle. For example, if everything you picked is embellished ball gowns, but you don't attend galas and balls every day, what features about those gowns can you carry over into your day-to-day style? The color? The embellishment? The drape of the gown? The material? Here's another example. Everything you picked is sporty casual with comic book character prints, but your office has a business professional dress code. You may not be able to wear a casual look, but you can pair up the superhero colors with a skirt and shirt for an outfit. Or perhaps you sport a necklace, bracelet, or belt with a superhero logo as one of your accessories. Or if your favorite character wears, let's say, cuffs on their wrists, you might sport wide bracelets as your way of acknowledging them. You can always find a way to incorporate your favorite fashion styles into your outfits, but sometimes you just have to be a little more subtle with how you do it instead of going head to toe with a specific look.

Fashion style is one component of personal style, but that does not mean that you have to pick only one fashion style as your personal style. If you are someone whose personal style is a fashion chameleon, then you will have multiple fashion styles in your wardrobe. However, the size of your wardrobe dedicated to each of these fashion styles may not be equal. When I worked in a setting with a business attire dress code, my wardrobe required a large collection of classic, preppy, or minimalist pieces. Since I worked 5 days per week, my preference for bohemian and sporty pieces had to wait until the weekends. With only 2 days per week to sport jeans and a peasant style blouse, I did not need many of these items in my wardrobe. Often when you prefer more than one fashion style, selecting 2—1 for work and 1 for days off— can work quite well. However, if you are someone who wants a small, tight capsule wardrobe, you will have to pick only one fashion style.

If the thought of assembling a vision board and filling out a quiz fills you with dread, I have another option to help ease you into the process of defining your fashion style. Look inside your laundry bin. The items that you are constantly washing week after week are the clothes that you most enjoy wearing. What stands out about them? Are they all jeans, soft knits, and T-shirts? Then start looking at outfits with these same features. Is everything a printed dress paired with a cardigan? Zero in on outfits with those 2 items. Your laundry bin not only holds the clues to what your fashion style is, it can also tell you what your dressing preference is, which is the second component of your personal style.

Personal Style Factor #2—Dressing Preference

When you get dressed in the morning, how do you do it? Do you start with a pair of boots because it's raining outside? Begin with a yellow shirt because you are feeling happy? Grab a pair of jeans because they are easy to work with? Can you even answer the question? Understanding your preferred dressing preference, ie, how you put together an outfit, can shed some light onto what you like for your personal style—complex, simple, or a combination of the 2.

At the same time, the way you organize your closet will help or hinder your ability to express yourself through your personal style. When your closet organization is aligned to your dressing preference, getting ready is quick and easy and the personal style that you show the world is consistent every day. Conversely, when your closet is out of alignment with your dressing preference, assembling an outfit for the day is difficult, takes a long time, and you'll probably end up walking out of the house sporting a random mess from one day to the next, leaving both you and your acquaintances wondering what your personal style really is.

If you couldn't answer my question on how you like to get dressed, the easiest way to figure this out is to take a look at how you organize your closet. Which brings up an important question: is your closet functioning well for you? Sometimes the problem with a wardrobe doesn't lie with owning too little or too much stuff, it's the fact that the way everything is stored is not right for you. That's one reason why dream closets are highly sought out, because when everything is arranged the right way, you can get dressed without a struggle.

Everyone assembles outfits differently. A closet organized by color may work well for one person, but a wardrobe arranged by item may be preferred by someone else. I often struggled with organizing my closet, because I didn't know which closet organization method was best for me. I've tried 5 different ways of organizing my closet—type, color, outfits, season, and occasion capsule—and discovered that each method has its pros and cons. As we review the different types of closet organizational styles and how they affect your dressing preference, you may learn about a new way to organize the clothes in your closet so that dressing every day is easier and faster for you.

Closet Organized by Type

A wardrobe arranged by type is the most common format you will see on home improvement shows and among retailers, both in the brick and mortar and online stores. All bottoms are together (jeans, skirts, shorts, trousers), all toppers are together (blazers, jackets, cardigans), all tops are together (knits, shirts, blouses, T-shirts), etc. When everything is arranged like this you'll see pretty fast how much (or how little) of something that you own. For myself it was very easy to see that I owned over a dozen pairs of jeans when they were all grouped together. This system works very well when you prefer to dress systematically and have function in mind. If it is a rainy day, I want to wear jeans tucked into boots. I go to the bottoms section, grab a pair of jeans and build the rest of my look from there. On a hot summer day I may want to sport shorts and a T-shirt, so I select my starting item and create an outfit around it. When someone has their closet arranged by type, their personal style has an element of simplicity and practicality to it, after all the weather and scheduled tasks of the day are driving their outfit decisions.

The second most common closet organization type is colors. All red pieces together, all blue pieces together, all prints together, etc. Once again, you'll often see this arrangement demonstrated by retailers and home improvement shows. After all, organizing by color is visually appealing. It's also not uncommon to see this type of organization paired with the first one, creating a system where items of the same type and color are grouped together. For example, all of the blazers are in one spot, and they go from light to dark colors.

When you dress by your mood of the day, a closet arranged by color is the perfect choice. Why? Because colors and moods go together. Feeling sad today? Select something from the gray and black section. In a happy mood? Just grab some bright colors. In addition to helping you dress by your mood, a closet arranged by color is a great way to identify when you have an excess of one color or another. When you have a closet that is half filled with black clothes: black jeans, black tops, black sweaters, black trousers, black blazers, it may make you pause and reconsider if you really want to add more black to your wardrobe.

Arranging a closet by color does have a downside. When I noticed a color was missing from my closet, I wanted to add it in, so that I would have more variety. It didn't matter that I never wore the color orange, I'd suddenly want an orange top because my sea of blues looked boring! If a person's dressing preference is driven by their mood, they are going to own a larger wardrobe with a lot of variety. Oftentimes the wardrobe will have multiple pieces in the same color (for example, a white blazer, trouser, shoes, and top) so that they are able to incorporate their favorite colors into their daily outfits. With the high variety in this type of wardrobe, the personal style here emphasizes variety and complexity, allowing the person to resemble a fashion chameleon, with outfits varying in both style and structure from one day to the next along with the person's mood.

Closet Organized by Outfits

When the time and energy to assemble outfits is limited, a closet storing a collection of pre-planned combinations is extremely helpful. When my closet was organized by outfits, I was able to grab and go. I didn't have to think about what to pair with what to put together an outfit. It was also easy to spot a wardrobe orphan. I enjoyed the utilitarian aspect of my closet when it was arranged by outfits, but there are 2 downsides. First, unlike the last 2 closet options, type and color, a closet arranged by outfits looks like a jumbled mess. Bottoms are mixed in with tops and the colors are spread out all over the place. Second, if you are someone who enjoys variety and creativity in your outfits, you may struggle to remix your clothes, because it's not that easy to see what you have when it's all jumbled together.

When someone has their closet arranged by outfits, their personal style has an element of consistency to it, they don't want to wear new outfit combinations all of the time. They've found the outfits they like best and are happy repeating them.

Closet Organized by Season

A wardrobe arranged by season has clear divisions among the clothes. This type of wardrobe is most common for someone who lives in a region of the world with changing weather patterns. For example, hot and dry in the summer and wet or snowy in the winter. In these cases the clothes are divided up, and oftentimes, only 1 or 2 seasons are kept in the working closet at 1 time. The rest is stored elsewhere. As someone living with 4 distinct climates, this was the closet style that I used for the longest time. Ironically, it was also the option that worked the least for me because I don't have a complex personal style. I used to box up my out-of-season clothes and store them outside of my working closet. At the start of each season I would devote multiple hours to swapping my clothes. Unfortunately, before this swap happened I would forget what I owned and often bought similar or even duplicate items. This behavior left me with many wardrobe repeats that would sit unworn throughout the season and turn into wardrobe orphans.

Dividing my wardrobe into seasons also considerably limited the use of my clothes. Since I live in a 4-season climate, and the weather is fairly consistent within each season, I only have about 3 months to sport my clothes before the weather changes. That means for 9 months, many items are going to sit unworn. Also, keeping out-of-season items out of sight severely reduced the creativity I could have with my wardrobe. If my summer dresses are packed away, I can't try to restyle them for fall with boots and a cardigan or blazer and tights. If winter clothes are stored, I don't have a sweatshirt handy for nights in the summer when it gets chilly outside or the air conditioning is set too low.

Similar to a closet arranged by color, when someone has their closet arranged by season, their personal style is often complex in nature, involving lots of change and variety, especially with prints and materials (for example, tweed and jewel tones in fall and pastels and flower prints for spring). Oftentimes this personal style has a maximal vibe to it (lots of colors, patterns, and textures) and incorporates the latest trends, because this person is constantly re-evaluating and updating their wardrobe as the seasons change.

Closet Organized by Occasion

A closet arranged by occasion capsules usually incorporates one of the other closet styles as well: type, color, outfit, or season. An occasion closet is the ultimate in order and structure, and the person normally has a very specific, defined sense of style. This is the person who somehow always seems to be dressed appropriately for every situation. And when your closet is arranged by occasion, this is very easy to do.

While every closet style has a specific dressing preference that pairs best with it, that doesn't mean that you can only have one dressing preference or one closet organization style. In fact, you probably don't. I know I don't. My personal closet is arranged first by occasion and then within each occasion by outfits. I like to be prepared for any event that comes up and I also like to grab and go without having to think about what I want to wear. But I don't stop there. I also rotate my clothes so that I can wear items with even frequency. Items near the door are to be worn first and after wearing and washing, they go to the back of the line for that category. Arranging my wardrobe by occasion first, by outfits second, and then rotating based on use, provides me with a functional working closet that satisfies my dressing preferences while meeting the goals for use of my wardrobe.

Your answer to the question "how do you get dressed" is a part of your personal style, which in its simplest form is either complex, simple, or a combination of the 2. The way that your closet is organized will help point you towards the answer. Another question that your closet can provide the answer to is what is your signature color.

Personal Style Factor #3—Signature Color

A signature color is the best shade for you. It reflects your personality and it's flattering for your complexion. It's the color that others think of when they think of you. So far, it sounds pretty simple right? Find one color that makes you feel like "you" and that's it, you are done.

Except analyzing colors is not always straightforward. The human eye can see approximately 7 million colors. That's a few more than what is found inside a Crayola® crayon box. And for each person, this color perception is different. To one person, certain colors and color combinations are soothing, while to others they are irritating. In addition to the difference in personal perception is the availability of a wide variety of colors in fashion. Since 2000, the Pantone Color InstituteTM has issued a color of the year. That's 16 colors at the time of writing this book. Additionally, a Pantone® Fashion Color Report is released biannually, for both the spring and fall fashion collections, respectively. These biannual guides announce a palette of 10 colors. That's 20 colors per year, or 200 colors over 10 years! Combine the large number of color options with the constantly changing landscape of what colors are "in season," and it's easy to see how someone can become confused as to what colors are their best colors, as well as how you can end up owning a wardrobe that is filled with lots of the wrong colors for you. So how do you weed through this mess and figure out what your signature color is?

Before we begin there's something about the phrase signature color that you need to know. You see, the phrase signature color is misleading because it implies that your entire wardrobe will consist of only 1 color. But for some people owning a wardrobe of only 1, 2, or even 3 colors is not very appealing. That's why when I'm talking about your signature color, I'm also going to discuss finding your signature color palette. The signature color palette is the group of coordinating colors that compliment your signature color. Knowing your signature color and signature color palette will allow you to exude a consistent personal style.

Color theory is a set of guidelines for how colors relate to each other as well as which combinations work best. The basic tool in color theory is the color wheel, which provides a visual representation of colors and color harmony. Selecting which colors are flattering on yourself can be broken down into the 3 main color groupings from the color wheel—primary, secondary, and tertiary. Primary colors are red, yellow, and blue, and these colors can't be mixed to form another color. Secondary colors are green, orange, and purple, and these colors are created from mixing the primary colors. Tertiary colors are created from mixing primary and secondary colors, giving these colors a 2-name designation: yellow-orange, red-orange, red-purple, blue-purple, blue-green, and yellow-green.

When you are trying to pinpoint what colors look best on you, trust your instincts. While shopping in a store, there is always a set of colors that you are attracted to. What are they? And where do they fall in the basic color wheel—primary, secondary, or tertiary? For example, my colors are: blue (primary color), purple (secondary color), and blue-purple (tertiary color). While I enjoy and wear other colors, these 3 colors are always the first ones to catch my eye, the colors that consistently make me feel amazing when I wear them, and the colors that generate the most compliments. These colors also accurately mimic my personality—calming (blue and purple). They are my signature colors.

Signature colors:
The colors you are drawn to again and again and again.

However, a wardrobe of only 3 colors would bore me, I want to branch out and include colors that I am not immediately attracted to, but I still want them to look good on me. To expand your colors you have to take your signature colors and build a color palette around them. Color palettes are often used for interior design and make-up selection. To design a color palette, select the colors that pair best with your signature colors. In your outfits, use the signature color as the primary color or the accent color for your looks. For example, my signature colors are blue and purple. Colors that pair well with blue and purple include yellow, red, and pink; core colors that pair well with blue and purple include white and brown.

All of these colors can make up my color palette. Then I simply decide if I want the signature color to be the focal point of my outfit, or the backdrop to my look. When the signature color is the focal point, I wear the blue as an accent piece, perhaps as a scarf or a pair of shoes. If the signature color is the backdrop, the larger pieces in my outfit (blazer, cardigan, top, trouser) are in shades of blue.

When considering what colors are your signature colors, you have to be aware of not only the color itself, but also the undertone of the color, warm or cool. Warm colors are associated with daylight and sunset and perceived as "exciting" (red/yellow side of color wheel), while cool colors are associated with grey or overcast days and perceived as "calming" (blue/green side of color wheel). An easy way to see which tone will work best on you is the mirror method.

Mirror method:
Do you look at your face or the garment first?

Use the mirror method to quickly and easily decide if the color of a garment is flattering on you. The mirror method consists of 5 steps:

1. Select 2 items of the same color, but with 2 different undertones, a warm version and a cool version.
2. Hold one item in each hand in front of a mirror, right for warm and left for cool.

3. Look away from the mirror. Return your gaze to the mirror, this time with the garment in your right hand near your face.
4. Observe where you looked first—was it at the item or at your face? Colors that are flattering will draw the attention TO the face. Colors that are not flattering will draw the attention AWAY from the face.
5. Repeat steps 3 and 4 with the garment in your left hand.

The mirror method will tell you which tone draws the observer's attention to your eyes or to your clothes.

Another option to design a personal color palette for yourself is to look at your physical attributes: skin tone, eye color, and hair color, and design your wardrobe based on a seasonal color palette. Pairing a seasonal color palette with a person's physical attributes is always used for make-up selection. Individuals are often grouped into 1 of the 4 seasons: spring, summer, fall, and winter (Table 7).

Table 7: *Seasonal Color Analysis*

Season	Quality	Preferred Colors
Winter	Blue or pink undertones to the skin, high contrast hair color, eye color and skin tone, sharp and striking	Intense rich colors or strong bright colors
Spring	Warm with golden undertones to the skin but subtle contrast	Soft warm colors
Summer	Blue and pink undertones to the skin, but very pale, low contrast hair color, eye color and skin tone	Soft neutrals and pastels, muted tones
Fall	Warm with golden undertones to the skin and lots of depth but not heavy contrast	Vibrant, warm, earthy colors

Once you know your personal color palette, you can weed out the clothes with colors that don't fit. Only owning the clothes that work best on you is one of the components of your personal style.

I've been discussing how to build a wardrobe around 1 signature color, with a corresponding color palette. When you want a small wardrobe, where everything goes with everything else, you'll want to limit your signature color to only one. But sometimes a person is equally drawn to 2 colors that don't pair well with each other. What do you do then? Simple. Your wardrobe will be split into 2 halves, one palette for each color.

Another aspect of your personal style is the neutrals that you use. Neutrals form the foundation for your wardrobe. What is the difference between a color and a neutral? That is a highly debated question. Some people would argue that colors absorb and reflect light to varying degrees, while neutrals either absorb all or block all of the light waves. A simpler explanation is that colors evoke an emotional reaction, while neutrals do not. In fashion, neutral colors include black, white, gray, brown, navy, cream, camel, olive, silver, and gold. They help expand the functionality of a wardrobe because neutrals are able to mix with any color.

While colors are lovely, your personal style doesn't have to include a signature color. You can make your mark by owning a wardrobe built around a palette of neutrals instead. Famous people with a neutral personal style include: Angelina Jolie, Jennifer Aniston, Kanye West, Bill Gates, and Audrey Hepburn. Each of these people are known for sporting a lack of color and not following the fashion trends in their daily outfits.

Personal Style Factor #4—Body Type

If you were to look at someone who feels good about their outfit or a person who is known for having a great sense of style, you'll see these people always have one thing in common—they understand fit. Dressing based on your body type requires an understanding of what silhouettes and materials will be most flattering on your own body. This knowledge allows you to pick clothes that account for the shape of your body, leading to outfits that enhance or camouflage whatever physical attributes you want.

Unfortunately, determining how to dress for one's body is often a challenge. The description of a person's physique ranges from shapes (rectangle, triangle, hourglass), to fruits (pear, apple, banana), to somatotypes (ectomorph, endomorph, mesomorph). With such a wide variety of labels applied to a person's body, it is easy to become confused. How do you figure out which type is for you? Simple. The common theme between physique and fashion body types is the classification of how adipose tissue is distributed on the body. A person is either slim, with a low accumulation of body fat (ectomorph), curvy with an uneven distribution of body fat (endomorph), or curvy with an even distribution of body fat and muscle (mesomorph) (Table 8).

Table 8: *Body Type and Body Shape Classification*

Physique Body Type	Fashion Body Type	Label	Clothing Features
Ectomorph Long, angular, thin, skinny, slim, slender	Rectangle, ruler/ banana, column, boyish, straight	Slim	Fabrics with natural draping and embellishments. Fitted cuts to soften the body and create curves
Endomorph Soft, large, round	Circle, oval, diamond, triangle, pear, apple	Curvy	Fabrics with weight to create structure. Cuts that create balance to emphasize the upper (for pear) or the bottom (for apple) halves
Mesomorph Lean, athletic, strong	Hourglass	Muscular	Fabrics with stretch and fitted cuts that define the waist

Limiting the classification of the human physique to only 3 options for body type and body shape provides 2 key pieces of information that you will use to dress yourself. You'll know what features of your body you want to show off or play down, and you'll know what shapes and fabrics will help you to achieve these goals. If you want to show off your shape, you'll need to look for clothes that don't fit well on a hanger, instead the clothes fit close to the body and have angles that highlight your curves (ie, curved hemlines, tapered waists, etc). When you want to hide your shape, you'll want the clothes to have the shape itself, and your body is the hanger.

Everyone is born with a specific body structure and shape. If an outfit looks lovely on the hanger but loses its appeal once worn on your body, the most likely culprit is the fit of the clothes. When it comes to looking good, it's not the size or the shape of your body that matters, it's how your clothes fit you. When you dress with your body type in mind, you exude an unspoken confidence that you understand your personal style.

Personal Style Factor #5—Lifestyle

Thus far we've looked at 4 factors that make up your personal style: fashion style, dressing preference, signature color, and body type. The last factor that affects your personal style is your lifestyle, ie, the way you live. All of the knowledge in the world about what you like, what looks good on you, and what fits you is useless if you can't actually wear any of it! When you review the factors that make up your personal style, you have to keep in mind that the choices that you make must be able to fit into your lifestyle.

For example, I adore the look of an outfit with a stiletto heel. The stilettos add height, portray confidence, become the focal point of an outfit, and let's face it, they're sexy. But my feet do not agree, they hate heels. Especially for the times when I do lots of walking, which is something that I do often. Despite my inner desire to wear stiletto heels every day, my feet and my lifestyle simply don't allow me to do so. Every time I wear a pair of thin, tall heels, I always end up swapping them out for flats, or walking around barefoot. Clearly my personal style can't include heels. If I'm constantly looking for outfits with heels, I'm going to end up very frustrated with my personal style. But I have an alternative, a wedge heel. The wedge gives me the height I need, can be paired with a platform bottom to reduce the strain on my feet, and the extra stability makes walking all day in them a breeze. My lifestyle and my feet demand a wedge heel over a stiletto heel, and my personal style reflects that. When you have a strong understanding of your personal style, you not only know what looks good on you, but you are able to wear it in your daily life.

Every day you have to put together an outfit, but it's only on certain days that you feel like "you" in your clothes. Those are the days when you feel like you hit the jackpot, and that's because your outfit is accurately representing your personal style. Understanding the features and elements that define your personal style also allows you to browse the retailers with a plan. You no longer have to wander the stores aimlessly hoping for a clue on what to purchase, nor do you have to waste countless hours trying on clothing that will never fit your body type or flatter your complexion. Once you have a clear picture of what you like, you are ready to tackle a shopaholic's favorite pasttime—shopping!

Chapter 5 recap:

Know the particular look that belongs only to you.

 Hit The Brakes:
Identify your personal style

- Use vision boards, quizzes, or your laundry bin to figure out your fashion style

- Look at how you get dressed in the morning, or how your closet is organized, to pinpoint if your personal style is complex, simple, or a combination of the 2

- Which colors you are naturally drawn to, either in the store or when comparing against your face in a mirror, are your signature colors

- Select clothes that flatter or conceal your body type to accurately reflect your style choices

- Showcase your personal style by adopting items that you can actually wear in your daily life

Understanding where your personal preferences fall among the 5 factors that make up your personal style— fashion style, dressing preference, signature color, body type, and lifestyle—has a considerable impact on your wardrobe. You'll know what to keep and what to toss while editing your closet, you'll know what to buy when you go shopping, and you'll feel more like "you" in your clothes.

Chapter 6

Let's go shopping!

Plan ahead to get the best results

Most retail stores have the same general layout. Near the entrance is often a table of perfectly folded clothes in multiple colors. As you move throughout the store you'll see that most of the merchandise is presented on hangers, grouped together by garment type, color, and size. If you watch where your feet are going, you'll probably find yourself walking in a circular or square pathway along a loop layout, with a grouping of displays that stop you along the way. The sales racks are always at the back of the store, along with the fitting rooms, and the sales register is often located somewhere in the middle of it all.

Store layouts are repetitive for a reason; retailers are well versed in how to persuade people to buy. When you visit a retail store you are going up against a team of professionals whose entire goal is to make you want to *buy, buy, buy.* Table-top displays, racks of clothes, the location of the fitting rooms and registers, all of it has been carefully planned to encourage a customer to purchase something. But the odds are not all stacked up against you. If retailers can map out a plan to get you to buy, then you can turn the tables and map out a plan on how you want to shop. Planning your shopping trip before you set foot inside a retail store enables you to walk away with what you *need*, and not with what retailers have convinced you to *want*.

Hit The Brakes:
Write a shopping list before you go to the store

Shopping with a list is often suggested in the context of grocery shopping, but I have found that shopping with a list is equally beneficial when I want to buy clothes. Shopping lists help you remember what you want to buy while at the store, saving you both time and money, and help to prevent impulse purchases. Shopping lists can be a useful tool for managing my wardrobe, but in order for the list to work best I must adhere to one important thing—I must create the list *before* I visit a retailer. Why?

The more time I spend visiting a retailer, the higher the temptation to acquire new items becomes. A retailer is filled with all of the items that I don't already own, but want to. This potential downfall means that a shopping list must be created *prior* to visiting a retailer. If I visit the stores to see what's available before I write my list, I'm going to include stuff based on what I see available, not based on what my wardrobe needs. I'll end up writing a list based on desire. When I write the list at home with my wardrobe in front of me, I am able to compose a list based on need, focusing on adding items that will fill the holes in my wardrobe. By establishing the ground rules in advance, I am able to stay on track when crafting my shopping list, without any outside distractions.

In order to craft an effective shopping list, you'll want to include the following 4 key areas: features, cost, quantity, and use. Let's take a closer look at each area.

Effective Shopping List Key Area #1—Features

What are the specifics about the item you are looking for?

The stores are always going to have items that I didn't know I wanted until I saw them. If my list simply states that I need a new dress, I'm going to wander around the stores looking at all of the dresses. I can easily grow distracted and start trying on dresses of various styles and colors and I may end up wanting a dress that doesn't really suit my needs. However, if I am specific about the attributes that the dress must have—blue print, A-line shape, machine washable, three-quarter length sleeves, fits into my existing business capsule— now I can weed out the dresses that do not meet all of the criteria I outlined in advance. Instead of aimlessly wandering the sales racks hoping something will jump out at me, I am able to quickly eliminate dresses that do not fit my requirements, and this enables me to zero in on the dresses that do. When you write a shopping list, remember to include as many of the following attributes as possible about the item that you need: material, fit, style, design, color, laundry care, and the wardrobe capsule you will add the piece to. The more specific your description is, the faster you can eliminate the things you do not need and zero in on the stuff you do.

Effective Shopping List Key Area #2—Cost

What is the price you want to spend on the item?

Deciding in advance how much to spend on an item is another way to help me to stay on track with my shopping, because I can once again weed through items quickly and eliminate those pieces that will put me over my budget. This also prevents me from walking away with guilt about a purchase because I spent more than I should have. This attribute is especially useful in blocking purchases that would have been made based on price tag persuasion.

Price tag persuasion is when the price of the item, and not the features of the item, leads to the purchase. Price alone doesn't dictate quality, longevity, or comfort. A $25 T-shirt may not last longer than a $5 T-shirt. A $100 sweater may be just as scratchy as a $10 sweater. In reverse, sometimes that $6 tank top will survive 100 washes and other times it will only last 2 washes. The price tag alone should never be the primary reason why I purchase an item, yet price is quite often the number one driver to do so. Too often in the past I've overpaid, because I thought the higher price tag automatically meant that it was a higher-quality item. Other times I've picked up something new because "it was a good deal" or because "it was on sale." Yet, despite the attraction of a low price, no matter how good the deal is, it's not a good enough reason for making the purchase. If I buy something new and only wear it one time before donating it, or I pick up a super cheap shirt because it was on sale and never wear it at all, then it really wasn't a good deal. Unworn and rarely used items become dust collectors, and when these seldom used pieces are donated, they are examples of wasted money.

A sale item is not a sale, if you're not going to use it. Unworn clothing is wasted money.

Remember, back in Chapters 3 and 4 you already weeded out all of the clothes that you aren't wearing from your closet. Your clothes have to earn their spot in your wardrobe and to be worthy of your hard earned dollars. Clothes must be purchases that you will wear, and not be stuff that merely becomes wardrobe orphans, delegated to the unused surplus of your wardrobe, waiting to be purged.

There are 2 things that you can do to help figure out how much you want to spend on something. First is to browse the retailers to get an idea of the average selling price. For some products, such as tank tops, you may see a small price range. For other products the price range may be very wide. A great example of this is jeans, which can range in price from $35 to $350. How do you decide how much to spend, especially when there is a wide price range to pick from? Calculate what you want the cost per wear (sometimes called the cost per use) to be. The cost per wear is attained through the formula below:

Cost per wear = purchase price ÷ number of times worn

The key to calculating the cost per wear of an item is knowing how many times you are going to wear it before you plan to get rid of it. When I started tracking cost per wear, I realized that frequency has a significant impact on whether I should spend or save on my purchase. The more often I wore an item, the lower the cost per wear became (Table 9).

Table 9: *Cost Per Wear*

Item	Purchase Price ($)	Times Worn	Cost per wear ($)
White Boyfriend Blazer	258.00	53	4.87
Denim Jacket	69.99	24	2.92
Black Boyfriend Blazer	99.90	16	6.24
Green Army Jacket	57.59	13	4.43

In Table 9 I had 2 toppers that have a cost per wear in the $4 to $5 range, the white boyfriend blazer and the green army jacket. The white boyfriend blazer was the most expensive item on my list, but it has also been worn the most, a surprising 53 times, bringing the cost per wear down to $4.87. The green army jacket was the least expensive item in the list and also the least worn, bringing its cost per wear to $4.43, relatively similar to the white boyfriend blazer, despite the difference in purchase price. In the future, I'll want to keep in mind that a white blazer gets a lot more use than a casual jacket, and if I want to spend a little more, the blazer is a better choice.

Here are a few more examples on how to decide when to spend and when to save based on cost per wear. I wear denim jeans almost every day. I'd say I wear denim jeans at least 95% of the time throughout the year. And I know from The DH Closet Challenge (Chapter 4), that I do not mind repeating the same pair of jeans within a week. Since my jeans have been established as a workhorse item, they are a core piece in my wardrobe. Wardrobe workhorse status is the driver for why I will comfortably spend up to $200 on one pair of premium denim jeans. Of course, if I see a pair of jeans that are not premium denim, I like the fit, style, and wash, and they are only $50, or $30, or $20, I'll purchase them too. But I'm willing to spend more on jeans, because they will get heavy use. And the heavier the use of the item will be, the more money I'm willing to put towards the purchase. I own a pair of premium denim jeans that cost me $150 dollars. I've had them for 2 years and at the time of writing this piece I have worn them 120 times. This means their cost per wear is down to $1.25.

A special occasion outfit is another time when I will spend a bit more, except this time, the cost per wear is going to stay rather high. After all, if I buy a new dress for a wedding, and I only attend 2 weddings that year, the dress is going to stay at a relatively high cost per wear. You need to keep this in mind when you're shopping.

A situation where I might want to spend a little less is on trousers. Since I rarely wear trousers over the course of the year, maybe only 3 or 4 times, I might want to focus on a lower-cost option, compared with what I'll spend on jeans. If the trousers cost is $100 and I will only wear them 4 times, I'm going to end up purging a pair of trousers with a cost of use of $25. But if I purchase trousers for $25 and I still only wear them 4 times, the cost of use by the time of purging will be $6.25. I especially like to do this when I want to test out a new trend or style. If the garment wears out and I find that I start wishing I still had the garment in my wardrobe, I'll consider spending a bit more on the replacement version.

You can use cost per wear to figure out when to spend a little more or a little less, but that's not the only information you can gather from cost per wear. If you track the cost per wear of your wardrobe over time, you'll also be able to pinpoint if the piece you bought became a wardrobe orphan or a wardrobe workhorse. A wardrobe workhorse is the clothing that you wear often. The garment is resilient and the materials and construction were done well and allow the apparel to be used a lot, resulting in a low cost per wear. When an item is able to last a long time, the likelihood that I will want to purchase from that brand again rises considerably. In contrast, a wardrobe orphan is the clothing that you don't wear often, either because the garment wasn't made well and the materials wore out really fast, or due to the fact that the item didn't fit your wardrobe needs or personal preferences. One exception to this rule is when something is bought for a specific event, for example a wedding or job interview. For these situations the item can be well made and suit the specific occasion, but the low frequency of these special events in one's daily life will lead to a garment that doesn't get worn very often.

Cost per wear is the key piece of information needed to decide how much I want to spend for something on my shopping list. If the item is something that I know I plan to wear often, or is for a special occasion, I may want to spend a little more. When the item is something that I don't think I'm going to wear a lot, I may want to spend a little less.

Effective Shopping List Key Area #3—Quantity

How many of the item do you need to purchase?

Deciding up front how many of something you want to purchase is a key decision to make before entering a store. This is especially important to decide when you are searching for an item that is hard to find or hard to fit. For myself, when I finally find that elusive item, I naturally want to purchase at least 2, just to eliminate having to hunt for it all over again in the future. But oftentimes, purchasing 2 can quickly turn into 4, 6, 8, or even more, especially when I am thrust into the situation where the clothing has been manufactured in lots of colors or patterns, or when the price is really reasonable. Difficult to fit and to find clothes can quickly lead to buying more than you need when the item is finally located.

A great example of this is a pair of nude ballet flats that I own. It was very difficult to find a neutral-colored ballet flat that flattered my skin tone and was comfortable on my fussy feet. When I finally found a pair, I immediately purchased 2 of them. My rationale at the time was that the shoes were so hard to find and to fit, I better have a backup. At the time of writing this book, I still haven't worn the second pair of ballet flats, and I bought them 2 years ago! How can this be? Simple. The problem is 2-fold: 1) I don't wear nude ballet flats very often and 2) the shoes are well made and they haven't worn out and needed to be replaced. At the time, buying 2 pairs seemed like a really good idea, but the longer the second pair of flats sits unworn in my closet, the more obvious it is becoming that I didn't really need to buy 2 at the same time after all.

I've talked about one example when buying duplicates didn't work, but that's not always the case, sometimes buying multiples does work. One of my favorite pieces to duplicate in my wardrobe is my layering knitwear, for underneath blazers and jackets. I'll usually purchase 2 at a time, in 2 different colors. And that's the key for why this works well for me, unlike the ballet flats where I purchased 2 of the same color, this time I bought 2 different colors. I'm able to wear both pieces in the same week, because they are not exact duplicates of each other.

How many you buy of something is a personal decision. For most of the clothes in my wardrobe, owning one is just enough. But for layering and the hard to fit items, my ideal number is 2 of the same style but in 2 different colors. When I'm shopping for something new, I take into account what I'm going to use the piece for. Knowing this in advance helps me plan if I want 1, 2, or more of something.

Effective Shopping List Key Area #4—Use

What outfit can I create with this item?

Clothes hang unused in a closet because you can't or aren't using them. And one reason for this is because you can't assemble the item into an outfit. Every day that you leave the house, you're wearing an outfit, therefore logic would dictate that everything that you buy should be outfit-centric. To avoid owning clothes that hang in the closet unworn, every new wardrobe addition has to either be an entire outfit or an item that will be paired with something that you already own to create an outfit. This means when you are writing your list you have to think about how you're going to wear the things that you want to buy.

Too often in the past I would walk into a store, see an item that I like, buy it, then bring it home and struggle to figure out how to wear it. The skirt was really cute in the store, but I don't own a top to pair with it. The wedge lace-up booties were in a really fun green and black plaid print, but everything in my closet is blue and white and doesn't pair with them. The blazer was gorgeous on the sales rack, but nothing in my wardrobe pairs with hot pink. The list goes on and on. When you write your shopping list, keep in mind that the stuff that you are buying will need to fit into an outfit for you to wear. Always shop with outfit combinations top of mind.

A shopping list will help you to stay focused on what you want to add to your wardrobe, but that's only one part of a wardrobe plan. Every time you buy something new, it is going to have an effect on your wardrobe. The other factor you have to decide is how often you want to focus on your wardrobe.

Hit The Brakes:
Decide how often you are going to shop for and edit your wardrobe

You have lots of choices on how often you want to do this: once per year, twice per year, at the start of each season, once per month, once per week, or even once per day. With so many options, how do you pick the right one for you? To do this, you have to take a look at your shopping style.

Shopping style is how often you enjoy shopping for clothes. Everyone falls into 1 of 2 group—you are either a gorge-style shopper or a graze-style shopper. Visiting a retailer to buy something new is exactly like sitting down to eat at a buffet: there's a lot of variety for you to pick from. Retailers present all of these options for a reason; they are trying to accommodate a wide variety of people to buy from their store. A buffet spread does the same thing—the host seeks to satisfy a wide variety of palates by providing lots of options.

Regardless of whether you are at a buffet or a retail store, the host is asking you to make a decision on how you will proceed, and you have 2 options: 1) take only what you like or 2) sample a little bit of everything. Shopping styles are the same way—some people gorge and others graze.

I have a close friend who shops for her clothes only twice per year. She's a busy gal, focused on juggling both her career and her family, and doesn't have the free time nor the desire to spend endless hours every week searching the stores for something new. When she shops, she dedicates an entire weekend to updating her wardrobe, and she only does this twice per year, in the spring (for spring and summer clothes) and in the fall (for fall and winter clothes). On those 2 weekends, she is 100% dedicated to her wardrobe. During those marathon sessions she edits her closet, confirms her personal style, plans her outfits for the upcoming seasons, shops for what she needs, and plans her outfits for her wardrobe capsules. The rest of the year her time is spent focusing on other matters. This is an example of gorge-style shopping. When you gorge at a buffet, you show up, load your plate high with only those things you know you enjoy, sit down to eat your meal, then move on to something else. Shopping gorge style does the same thing, with clothes instead of food.

Gorge-style shopping provides the obvious advantage of saving time. A person's wardrobe is the main focus for only 2 or 4 days out of the entire year. Once the wardrobe has been re-evaluated and updated for the season, it doesn't need attention again until the weather has changed. In addition to saving time, a gorge-style shopper typically owns a carefully curated wardrobe. This is due to the extensive focus that is placed on the individual's wardrobe for a short period of time. Shopping only a handful of times per year forces one to closely examine their wardrobe needs and function. Outfits must be planned, and any wardrobe holes are identified and filled, because there is a limited window of time to shop. For gorge-style shoppers, there is no "oh I'll finish shopping for this outfit later," and there is no continued cycle of purchasing and returning. Everything added to the wardrobe has been carefully selected and its place established up front. Additionally, by purchasing many garments at the same time, it is easier to purchase a color palette where all of the shades will coordinate well, because all of the pieces are from the same retail season and the same dye lots. If this sounds like you, then you are a gorge-style shopper.

Of course, gorge-style shopping is not for everyone. Since gorge-style shoppers are purchasing a lot of stuff at one time, there is the potential to trigger the feast or famine response, "I better get it before it's gone," leading to purchasing more than what is really needed. Also, the large amount of time dedicated to both wardrobe management and the act of shopping itself, as well as the large number of new clothes and shoes added at one time, may be too overwhelming for some people.

I am one of those people who is typically left dazed and confused when trying to consolidate all of my wardrobe planning and shopping into a mere 2 or 4 sessions per year. Marathon sessions where I shop or edit my closet for more than 4 hours at a time don't work for me. Long hours dedicated solely to my wardrobe cause me to lose focus and I start making impulse decisions. I also have a constantly evolving style and I like lots of choices. If any of this sounds like you, then you are probably not a gorge-style shopper either—you and I are graze-style shoppers.

A graze-style shopper enjoys updating their wardrobe often. I learned during The DH Closet Challenge (Chapter 4) that I enjoy making little tweaks to my wardrobe throughout the season. A new top here, a swap of a jean style there, these mini refreshers make me feel more "of the moment" with my style, while giving me less stress when making a purchasing decision. As a graze-style shopper, I'm only faced with the task of 1 or 2 purchasing decisions at a time, instead of 10 or more. My sessions with my wardrobe are short; I don't have to spend countless hours at a time in the retail stores or editing my closet. I have the freedom to slowly adjust my working closet over the course of the season, constantly turning over a small number of clothes and shoes at a time. If this sounds like you, then you are also a graze-style shopper.

Both gorge- and graze- shopping styles can work very well. But you have to select the right shopping style for you. Reviewing the shopping style worksheet below, select yes or no to see what your shopping style is (Figure 5).

Figure 5: *Shopping Style Worksheet*

Question	Yes	No
1. I grow overwhelmed when forced to make lots of decisions at one time		
2. I enjoy change		
3. I like to shop for multiple days at a time		
4. I find it easy to focus for hours at a time		
5. My personal style reflects the latest trends		
6. I quickly get bored with my clothes		
7. I prefer to change the colors and patterns of my clothes to reflect the current season		

If you answered yes to 4 or more of the statements in the shopping style worksheet, you are a graze-style shopper. If you answered no to 4 or more of the statements in the shopping style worksheet you are a gorge-style shopper. Knowing how you shop is your clue for when you should shop. If you try to shop against your shopping style, you are going to end up making impulse purchases and find it difficult to edit your wardrobe. If you shop in agreement with your shopping style, then the things that you buy will be more in line with your wardrobe needs and preferences, and editing your closet will be easy. To successfully manage your wardrobe, you have to know when you are going to spend time with your wardrobe: once per year, twice per year, at the start of each season, once per month, once per week, or daily.

Another key to managing your wardrobe is deciding what you are going to do with the new stuff that you buy. It doesn't matter if you buy a little (graze shopper) or a lot (gorge shopper) when you buy something new, you need to decide what impact you want it to have on your wardrobe. Do you want to increase the size of your wardrobe, decrease the size of your wardrobe, or maintain its current size?

Increasing the size of your wardrobe is easy, simply keep adding things in as you buy them. This often happens when you do something to change your lifestyle, such as taking up a hobby that requires a new capsule wardrobe. But unless you have limitless closet space, sooner or later you are going to have to make the decision to start maintaining the size of your wardrobe or to decrease its size. When you find yourself faced with a closet filled with too much clothing, you can use any of the closet editing tips in Chapters 3 and 4 to reduce its size. And when you want your wardrobe to stay the same size then you have to one in/one out your purchases (ie, remove one item for every new item that you add).

Thus far in this chapter I've discussed how you put together both a shopping list and how often you plan to manage your wardrobe, but there is one more aspect about owning a wardrobe that I'd like to mention—how to transition your wardrobe. Sometimes lifestyle needs change; a few examples include: you go from working in a business setting 5 days per week to being a stay-at-home mom, you've graduated from school and started working your first corporate job, and you've retired from the work force and now go on cruises as part of your retirement. Other times it's not the life events that spark a change in your wardrobe, it's your own preferences. You've owned a wardrobe with 2 core colors and now you want only one, you've decided that you want to change your personal style from bohemian to sporty, or you simply hate everything that you own and want a clean slate. Regardless of the reason, in all of these cases you are not looking to maintain your wardrobe, you need to overhaul it.

The logical course of action to overhaul a wardrobe is to decide what your new occasion capsules are (Chapter 2), how much stuff you need for each one (Chapter 4), and what your personal style is (Chapter 5), then simply clear everything out and buy it all new. But for most people, including myself, doing that is impossible. You don't have the money, the time, or the desire to make that big of a change all at once. What you need to do instead is to transition your wardrobe over time.

Transitioning your wardrobe can be broken down into 2 parts: what you have and what you need. First, you want to review the clothes that you already own and see if any of them will work for your new needs. For example, if you worked in a corporate setting and one of your outfits consisted of blazer, blouse, and trousers, can any of these pieces be mixed with jeans for a more casual look? Or can the blouse be added to a tuxedo pant for a dinner on a cruise? If you wore tunic sweaters, jeans, and tall boots to class, can you pair the tunic sweater with a skinny leg trouser and heels or the jeans with a blazer and flats for a new job? Reworking what you already own, you may discover some wardrobe holes, items that you need to buy that will make your current clothes work for your new lifestyle needs.

If you have an outfit that you hate, is there anything about the outfit that is salvageable? For example, if your outfit is a jacket, mockneck top, skinny jeans, and heels, would you like it better if you paired the jacket with a scoopneck knit, skinny jeans, and short boots? If you always wear a waist length, crewneck, button-front cardigan with a blouse and trousers, would a different style cardigan (hip length, open front, curved hem, etc) refresh the look? Once again, critically analyzing your current outfits for what you can do to make them feel fresh and new will help you transition your wardrobe over time. After you've worked with what you have, then you can move on to adding new things.

In this chapter I've covered a lot of areas that make up your plan for your wardrobe. The Shopping Plan Worksheet summarizes these ideas for you and can act as your guide to shopping for your wardrobe. Unlike the shopping list mentioned earlier The Shopping Plan Worksheet not only covers each item's cost and physical features, it also includes the rationale and impact to your wardrobe (Figure 6). When you know the answers to all of these questions before you buy something, you can ensure that what you bought was a wise decision for your wardrobe.

Hit The Brakes:
Use the Shopping Plan Worksheet to help manage your wardrobe

Figure 6: *Shopping Plan Worksheet*

1.	Why are you shopping?
2.	Can you use the clothes that you have? If you answer no to this question, you can skip Question 3.
3.	Then why are you buying new clothes?
4.	What are you trying to accomplish with this purchase?
5.	What are the features the garment must have?
6.	How often will you use the clothes (or need the outfit)?

| 7. Will you use the clothes for anything else? |
| 8. What do you think you need? |
| 9. Did you browse for the items? If your answer is no, do not proceed to the next question until you do. |
| 10. What are reasonable prices that you would like to spend on the items after your research? |
| 11. Are you comfortable spending this? If your answer is no, revise your price range until you are comfortable. |
| 12. Do you need to remove anything from your current wardrobe to make room for the new items? |
| 13. What are you going to do with the unwanted clothes? |

I'm going to explain the 4 areas of the shopping plan a little closer, then I'll show you the plan in action, using 2 case studies. When you are working through the answers to these questions before you shop for yourself, remember to use the information that you've collected up to this point in this book: what your wardrobe capsules are (Chapter 2), how much stuff you need in each capsule (Chapter 4), and what your personal style is (Chapter 5).

A Closer Look at the Shopping Plan—Rationale

The first 4 questions of the Shopping Plan Worksheet focus on the rationale, the reason for why you are going to buy something new. These questions have been designed to bring awareness to your shopping trip. To answer these questions, you need to be aware of what is already inside your closet (Chapter 2).

Rationale Questions:

1. **Why are you shopping?** Distinguishes if your intent for your shopping trip is based on need or want; also,

for need-based items, establishes what wardrobe capsule and outfit the item will be used for.

2. **Can you use the clothes that you have?** Points out if there is something inside your closet you can use instead of buying something new. If you answer no to this question, you can skip Question 3. You'll answer no when there is a genuine wardrobe hole in your closet (ie, you cannot use what you already own). Common events that usually lead to shopping for something new include: special occasion (wedding, graduation, baby shower, bridal shower, funeral, new job, and retirement) as well as the following situations: new hobby, injury, pregnancy, and clothing wore out. If you answer yes to this question, move on to Question 4.

3. **Then why are you buying new clothes?** Brings clarity to the reason why you are adding to your wardrobe when you already have something you can use instead.

4. **What are you trying to accomplish with this purchase?** The explanation for why you are buying something new for your wardrobe.

Once you've established why you are going shopping and the wardrobe hole you are seeking to fill, you'll move on to the next set of questions to establish what features you want the item to have.

A Closer Look at the Shopping Plan—Item and Cost

The physical attributes of the item itself, as well as the cost, can be pulled from your shopping list earlier in this chapter. In the Shopping Plan Worksheet, zeroing in on the exact features of what you want is the objective of Questions 5 to 8. To answer these questions, you need to be aware of the amount of use you want for your new item (Chapter 4) as well as what your personal style is (Chapter 5).

Item Questions:

5. **What are the features the garment must have?** Pinpoint the material, fit, style, design, color, laundry care, and wardrobe capsule for the item in order for it to work with your current wardrobe and style.

6. **How often will you use the clothes (or need the outfit)?** Brings attention to how much use you will get out of this item, which will drive how much you want to spend as well as the potential cost per wear of the item.

7. **Will you use the clothes for anything else?** Assess the potential for the item to be used with the clothes you already have in your closet.

8. **What do you think you need?** Exactly what are you looking for in one sentence. Remember that everything that you buy you should be able to assemble into an outfit. If you are shopping for a missing piece for something in your closet, or you are shopping for an outfit and you only bought half of it in one store, be sure to keep the pieces with

you so that you can make sure it really works before you buy it.

Clearly defining what you want before you shop helps save time in the stores. When you know what you are looking for, you can ignore all of the items that surround you that do not fit what you planned to buy.

How much you want to spend is the focus of Questions 9 to 11. Knowing how much you want to spend before you go to the stores will help to prevent becoming persuaded to buy something because it's on sale.

Cost Questions:

9. **Did you browse for the items?** You don't know what's available and what a reasonable price is until you've taken a look at what's available to buy. Browsing for an item is how you do your research and learn a general idea of what a reasonable price is for what you want. You cannot move on to Question 10 until you have answered yes to this question and done your research on product availability and price points.

10. **What are reasonable prices that you would like to spend on the items after your research?** After you've done your research on what the average price is for what you want, you can use this information to decide what the cost per wear of the item will be. With this information you can decide on a price range that you are comfortable spending.

11. **Are you comfortable spending this?** If your answer is no, revise your price range until you are comfortable.

With three-quarters of the shopping plan complete, rationale, item, and cost, only one final consideration is left—what you are going to do with your current wardrobe because you added something new.

A Closer Look at the Shopping Plan—Impact

What you are going to do to manage your wardrobe is the focus of the last 2 questions.

Impact Questions:

12. **Do you need to remove anything from your current wardrobe to make room for the new items?** If you have found the ideal number of items you want for your wardrobe (Chapter 4), you need to decide if you want to increase your wardrobe's size, or maintain it. You'll increase its size if you do not remove something from your closet when you purchase something new. Additional factors that cause your wardrobe to creep up in number are discussed in Chapter 8).

13. **What are you going to do with the unwanted clothes?** Decide what you want to do with your old stuff. A few options for your unwanted clothes are covered in Chapter 3.

Now I'm going to put the Shopping Plan Worksheet into action with 2 examples, creating a new wardrobe capsule (Figure 7) and adding to an existing wardrobe capsule (Figure 8).

Andrew just joined a gym, and needs to create a workout capsule for his wardrobe. This will be a new occasion capsule for his wardrobe.

Figure 7: *Shopping Plan Example #1: Andrew's Working Out*

1. Why are you shopping?   *I started going to the gym and I need clothes to work out in.*
2. Can you use the clothes that you have?   *Yes.*
3. Then why are you buying new clothes?   *Because the clothes that I have are functional, but they do not represent the style I want for the gym.*
4. What are you trying to accomplish with this purchase?   *I want outfits I look good in, feel confident in, and are functional for working out at the gym.*
5. What are the features the garment must have?   *Loose fit, comfortable, deep pockets, full range of motion, and colors of black, gray, and light gray. I need tops, shorts, and sneakers.*
6. How often will you use the clothes (or need the outfit)?   *Twice per week = 2 outfits. But I do laundry once per week and always want an outfit that is clean, therefore 3 outfits.*
7. What do you think you need?   *3 T-shirts, 2 shorts, 1 pair of sneakers.*
8. Will you use the clothes for anything else?   *Yes. Lounge wear. Sneakers can be paired with jeans for running errands on weekends.*
9. Did you browse for the items?   *Yes.*

10. What are reasonable prices that you would like to spend on the items after your research?
T-shirts $25 to $40. Shorts $30-$45. Sneakers $75 or less
11. Are you comfortable spending this?
Yes.
12. Do you need to remove anything from your current wardrobe to make room for the new items?
For the clothes no, this is a new occasion capsule for my wardrobe.
13. What are you going to do with the unwanted clothes?
For the sneakers, my old sneakers will go into the trash bin.

Using the shopping plan, Andrew was able to purchase 3 T-shirts, 2 pairs of shorts, and 1 pair of sneakers. He has 3 outfits for his new workout wear capsule.

Marie owns an outfit without a top. The outfit is a brown suede jacket, a pair of bootcut jeans, and brown cowboy boots. This outfit is part of her current fall capsule wardrobe.

Figure 8: *Shopping Plan Example #2: Marie's Filling In*

1. Why are you shopping?
I have an outfit that's missing a top.
2. Can you use the clothes that you have?
No.
3. Then why are you buying new clothes?
N/A, there are no clothes in my wardrobe that will serve this purpose.
4. What are you trying to accomplish with this purchase?
I want to complete an outfit.

5. What are the features the garment must have?
The top needs to fit underneath the brown suede jacket, the color has to flatter my skin tone, and go with the jacket. Potential colors include: ivory, black, navy, orange, and green. After comparing colors that have the potential to pair well with brown, against the jacket itself, ivory was selected.

6. How often will you use the clothes (or need the outfit)?
Once per week.

7. What do you think you need?
One ivory top that pairs with the brown suede jacket.

8. Will you use the clothes for anything else?
No.

9. Did you browse for the items?
Yes.

10. What are reasonable prices that you would like to spend on the items after your research?
$25 to $40

11. Are you comfortable spending this?
Yes.

12. Do you need to remove anything from your current wardrobe to make room for the new items?
No, the top is to complete an outfit.

13. What are you going to do with the unwanted clothes?
N/A, adding something new to my wardrobe.

Using the shopping plan, Marie brought her brown suede jacket to the stores to try out various options. Ultimately she was able to purchase one ivory top that was used to complete her outfit.

Over time, completing the Shopping Plan Worksheet will become second nature to you. When you map out a plan on how you want to shop, and you walk into a store with a list that clearly describes what you want to buy, you'll increase your chances of avoiding making an impulse purchase. You'll also raise the likelihood that you walk away from a store with the stuff that you need, and not with what retailers have convinced you to want.

Unfortunately, sometimes even the best laid plans hit a speed bump, and you unintentionally buy something on impulse. The reasons why and how to stop it are coming up in the next chapter.

Chapter 6 recap:

Know what you want before you buy.

Hit The Brakes:
Write a shopping list before you go to the store

• Before you shop, know the features, cost, quantity, and use for the item you are looking for. You don't have to shop for an entire outfit every time, but everything that you buy must be able to pair into an outfit with something in your closet

Hit The Brakes:
Decide how often you are going to shop for and edit your wardrobe

• Choose if you want to review and shop for your wardrobe once per year, twice per year, once per season, once per month, once per week, or daily

• Before adding something new, decide if you want to increase the size of your wardrobe, decrease the size of your wardrobe, or maintain its current size.

To *increase* wardrobe size, keep adding new things.
To *decrease* wardrobe size, remove more than you add.
To *maintain* wardrobe size, add and remove the same number of items

Hit The Brakes:
Use the Shopping Plan Worksheet to help manage your wardrobe

• The Shopping Plan Worksheet brings awareness to these 4 key areas:

1. Clearly define why you are shopping
2. Understand exactly what you are looking for
3. Decide how much you want to spend
4. Know what effect the new wardrobe addition will have to your closet

Managing a wardrobe requires you to be aware of what you are doing with your clothes, both when you want to add something new and when you are reviewing what you own over time.

Chapter 7

Learn how to succeed when you shop

Shop mindfully, not mindlessly

Have you ever looked at something inside your closet and asked yourself "why did I buy that?" I think we all say this sooner or later. You find yourself out shopping at the mall, or on the web, or maybe even while on vacation, and you suddenly stumble upon something that you just have to have in your life. What do I normally do in this situation? I snatch it up, of course! But why do we sometimes buy things that we rarely, or never, actually use?

Everyone goes shopping for one of 2 reasons: we *want* it or we *need* it. For some people, shopping for clothes is always to fill a need. The person shops to address a genuine wardrobe hole. If they don't need it, they don't buy it, end of story. It doesn't matter if the item fits well, is a flattering color, is a fair price, or simply makes them happy when they put it on. If the item is not essential or important for their lifestyle, if it's not going to serve an immediate purpose, if it doesn't fit into their personal style, then it's simply not purchased. Often men are stereotyped as shopping like this for their clothes, but some women do as well.

However, as an ex-shopaholic, when I went shopping for clothes it was an entirely different matter. Addressing a need is no longer the goal, instead shopping is used to support a want, a desire to possess something. In Chapter 1, I mentioned that one of the key elements of shopping was emotional motivation; you shop to escape, you shop to reinvent, you shop to be accepted. When you go shopping without a plan, you're going to end up shopping based on emotional motivation, and you'll find yourself walking away with stuff that you bought on impulse. Now sometimes an impulse purchase actually works out, and becomes a beloved item in your wardrobe. But more often than not, the impulse item becomes a wardrobe orphan, and buying it was a waste of your time and your hard-earned money.

Impulse shopping happens to everyone, but that doesn't mean that you can't do something about it. The tools mentioned in the last chapter—shopping with a list and creating a plan to manage your wardrobe—will help you to become more mindful about what you are shopping for, as well as how to maintain your wardrobe over time. But sometimes having lists and plans is not enough. As an ex-shopaholic I can tell you first hand just how difficult was is to stop shopping even when I knew that I should. It's like there was some inner force that was compelling me to buy something, despite common logic telling me not to. How does someone conquer a force that is motivating them from the inside? Is it even possible to do so?

Yes, it is. To conquer my addiction to shopping, first I had to know what was really causing it, then I had to work on changing my behavior over time so that I walked away from a retailer with a different result.

To understand what causes someone to impulse shop, I'm going to take a look inside the brain, or more specifically 3 chemicals that are inside the brain that can lead to emotional shopping: dopamine, serotonin, and noradrenalin. These 3 brain chemicals, or neurotransmitters, are chemical messengers that transmit information throughout the brain and the body. The first neurotransmitter, dopamine, plays a major role in reward-driven behavior. Dopamine levels are raised when you experience something pleasurable. The second neurotransmitter, serotonin, regulates moods and emotions. Low serotonin levels lead to depression. The third and final chemical messenger, noradrenalin, is in charge of keeping you safe and triggers the flight, fight, or freeze response. High noradrenalin levels lead to anxiety. An imbalance in any 1 of these 3 neurotransmitters will affect your behavior. In this case, shopping mindlessly, which is why you walk out of a store with an impulse purchase.

I'm going to look at each neurotransmitter and how it affects shopping behavior one-by-one, using myself as the example. I'll start with dopamine. Dopamine-producing drugs are often highly addictive. Over time, a user will develop a tolerance to the drug, and require more, and more, and more drug, to produce the same effect. Why? As more dopamine is flooded into the body from the drug, the body starts to produce less and less of its own dopamine. With the body's natural dopamine levels low and no longer producing a response, the user will have to rely on the drug to provide the effect. In the case of shopping addiction, dopamine is released at levels higher than normal after the shopper buys something; this act produces the same sensations as if the person had taken a dopamine-producing drug. A shopaholic goes shopping seeking to make a purchase, which releases dopamine, leading to feeling good, which supports more shopping.

Shopping → Purchase → Dopamine → Pleasure → Shopping

The pleasure experienced after making a purchase suggests that it is OK to buy something. I want to feel pleasure, and if buying something will lead to that feeling, I want to do it again. Constantly seeking a "rush" or "thrill" following the act of buying an item is often called the shopper's high.

I've spent years sneaking in my shopping trips in pursuit of the shopper's high. During these hours of searching for that elusive perfect item, I transformed into the modern-day huntress, with only one objective in mind:

Search → Stalk → Buy

I would search high and low, leaving no retail store unturned as I sought out my perfect item. And once I found what I wanted, the journey did not stop there. Nope, I simply moved on to the next phase, stalking. When I didn't like the price, my inner predator stalked my prey, just like a large cat in the jungle. I would check in weekly, daily, maybe even hourly, awaiting the crucial moment when the price dropped. And sooner or later, it typically did and then it was time to pounce and I would buy the item.

Buying something at a price lower than the original selling price is exhilarating. Couple that feeling with the reward for my patience, and I emerge with my new purchase feeling elated. My chest puffs out with great pride at acquiring my new kill, ahem, I mean new purchase. In today's day and age of convenience, I no longer need to hunt for food or shelter. But the drive to search, find, and take, is still strong. Shopping became my outlet for this instinct-driven behavior. Did any of that sound familiar? No, that's OK, because we have 2 more neurotransmitters to look at.

Sometimes a shopping trip is not driven by dopamine and the need to feel pleasure. Instead you go to the stores for the exact opposite reason, you're feeling depressed, which is due partly to serotonin. The link between serotonin and depression has come under scientific debate in recent years, because the drugs that raise serotonin levels may raise the levels of other chemicals as well. Additionally, while these drugs have helped many people to overcome their depression, there are also many people whom these drugs don't help. The latest clinical research suggests that depression is not a "one size fits all" condition. Depression may be caused by more than one mechanism. If this is true, it may help to explain why people can suffer from different types of depression. And why for some individuals, drugs that raise serotonin levels are ineffective.[8]

While serotonin's involvement in depression continues to undergo scientific debate, there is no denying that an association exists between serotonin and depression in certain individuals. For the sake of this book, and simplicity, I'm going to adhere to the concept that low serotonin levels lead to depression. When I was feeling sad, miserable, unhappy, blue, or just down in the dumps, I would shop. If this also sounds like you, then you should know that it's not the dopamine and the thrill of the hunt that's motivating you, it's serotonin and depression. Adding to this complexity is the fact that when you're depressed and you go shopping, you may end up making 1 of 2 types of purchases:

1. Clothes that reinforce depression
2. Clothes to alleviate depression

A person who is shopping because they are seeking to reinforce the depression uses the fact that they bought something new as a reason to continue to feel

[8] Healey D. Editorial: serotonin and depression. *BMJ*. 2015;350:h1771.

miserable. When I was depressed shopping, sometimes I wanted to keep the negative feelings of hopelessness, emptiness, numbness, and helplessness. Maybe I didn't think I deserved better. I couldn't see the silver lining of a situation. I just got so used to feeling depressed that I began to think that's how I should always feel, and it became a habit to feel that way. So I shopped as a penalty for my crimes, in this case feeling depressed, to reinforce continuing to feel this way. And my purchases would reflect my mood. None of the items were pieces that I could use or enjoy. Colors were wrong for my skin tone, the fit of garments was not flattering, and materials were uncomfortable. But everything helped me continue to feel bad about myself.

On the flip side, sometimes I would try to cheer myself up or shake off my depressed moods by shopping for new items. Now the goal of my shopping excursions was to alleviate the depression and have the negative mood and emotions go away. In these cases, my purchases were full of colors, styles, and materials that were flattering on me. And while the new addition would make me happy when I found it, tried it on, purchased it, and brought it home, eventually the depressed mood would return. When this occurred I'd be off to shop once again to squash the depressed feeling like a bug, even if it would only last for a short period of time.

If the first 2 scenarios don't sound familiar to you, maybe the one based on the third and final neurotransmitter, noradrenalin, will. Sometimes when you shop you aren't interested in feeling happy or sad. Another mental state may be involved, stress and the need to feel safe, which is driven by noradrenalin. During the times when I felt compelled to ponder a stressful situation, I went shopping. My cat had fallen gravely ill and did not have a positive long-term outcome. A beloved family member passed away. A conflict with a friend or loved one came up. I had a rough day work. I'd been in a car accident. Any of these situations would place me into panic mode.

Shopping sessions due to stress were focused more on the experience than on the purchases themselves. My time in the stores was my alone time. I was able to do something that felt "normal" when I was surrounded by chaos in my life. I could blow off steam by focusing on searching for something, instead of dealing with upsetting situations. These purchases were haphazard in nature. Sometimes I liked them, other times I did not. Sometimes they were flattering, and other times they were not. There was no rhyme or reason to the things that I purchased; buying something was merely a way to blow off some steam and give myself a time out while I worked to put my mind and soul back into balance. During times of high stress, some people meditate or work out, but for me, I would go shopping.

In the beginning of this chapter I stated that everyone goes shopping because they *want* it or because they *need* it. If you've ever come across something in your closet that you couldn't believe you even bought to begin with, that is because you shopped based on *want* and not *need*. And that want-driven behavior was stimulated by your neurotransmitters: dopamine, serotonin, or noradrenalin.

The logical solution to overcome an addictive behavior is to just stop doing it. In the case of shopping addiction, just stop shopping. However, if you are addicted to shopping and have struggled to change your shopping ways, then I don't need to tell you that trying to quit cold turkey doesn't always work, especially when emotions are involved. Changing your behavior is often very difficult to do. It was something that I personally struggled with for a long time.

The reason why wishing to change my shopping ways never worked was because overshopping is not a one size fits all action. Many motivations can lead to overshopping—pleasure, depression, stress, etc. With more than one potential cause, how can you ever hope to change your shopping habits?

In the field of psychology the answer would be Cognitive Behavioral Therapy (or CBT), which is a fancy 3-word term to describe a short-term, hands-on approach to changing your behavior. But I have another fancy 3 words that I like better to describe what I'm about to tell you to do: confrontation and desensitization (or CAD).

No matter what you call it (CBT or CAD), the general idea is the same—look at the pattern and behavior that you currently have, then set goals to change it. In Chapter 1 you took a look at where you fell within each of the 4 key elements of shopping; I told you that those numbers could serve as a baseline value. The data you gathered then is where you start. Everything that you do in this chapter can be compared against where you started, so that you can see your progress.

To retrain yourself for future shopping sessions you have to confront all of the emotional shopping drivers (dopamine, serotonin, and noradrenaline) and then reprogram your brain so that you are desensitized during your shopping sessions. By changing how your brain interprets the act of shopping and making a purchase, shopping and buying stuff will no longer provide the emotional payoff that it used to. Shopping will no longer be another mindless part of your daily routine; instead when you go shopping you will be aware of what you're doing and the consequences of your actions.

It is not an easy process to retrain your brain; it certainly wasn't easy for me. You're going to make mistakes along the way, and when you do, hop on over to Chapter 9 for some tips on how to get back on track when you step out of bounds. It might not be easy, but I encourage you to keep pushing along down the pathway to change. It took me a while, but over time I finally learned to proceed in a state of mindfulness of my actions when I shopped, instead of wandering around the retailers mindlessly. And in general, I began to shop less overall because shopping no longer provided the benefit that it used to. Shopping simply became an act for me to buy stuff when I needed to, instead of an act that was driven by my emotional wants and desires. If you've been struggling with changing your shopping behavior, maybe one of the following tips that worked for me will be helpful for you too.

Hit The Brakes:
Before you shop ask yourself "why am I here?"

The definition of shopping is to go to a store to purchase goods. Sounds pretty basic, right? There's nothing in the definition of shopping to suggest that any emotions are required. But as I mentioned earlier, impulse shopping is driven by your emotions. That's why you have to bring the emotional reason front and center when you want to shop. And the way to do this is to ask yourself "why."

Back in Chapter 1 you used the "why" question to learn your emotional motivation for shopping. Now the "why" question has returned. Ask yourself "why am I here?" every time you find yourself in a store (either in person or online). The reason for this is so that you recognize what type of shopping you are there to do. When I did this I discovered that many times I would go into the stores to shop because I was looking for an emotional release, not for a specific item. I was in the store because I *wanted* something, not because I *needed* something.

Asking yourself what reason sent you to the store to begin with lets you set the expectation in advance as to what you want to get out of the shopping experience during that visit. Once you know why you are there, you can then set the goal for the shopping visit. If I am in the store because "I want some me time" then I am free to browse, but I am not free to purchase. When I am in the store to "see what's new and in style" again I am free to browse, but not to make a purchase.

Asking yourself "why" doesn't stop once you know why you are in the store and the goal of that trip. You have to constantly repeat the question throughout your shopping visit. A shopaholic has an inner drive to shop, and it is not silenced when you enter a store, it's amplified. The more time you spend visiting a retailer, the more stuff that you pile into your shopping cart, the more stuff that you try on, all of these actions lead you down the pathway to buy something. As you walk along this path, you have to repeat the question, often, so that you remain focused.

Questioning yourself becomes your new shopping mantra, forcing you to focus on why you are in the store, instead of getting distracted by the allure of all these shiny, new things that surround you. Curious what you might find out? For myself, 9 times out of 10 when I was visiting a retailer, I was not seeking to fulfill a wardrobe need; I was trying to fill an emotional hole that fit into 1 of the following 5 buckets: reward, stress buster, alone or "me" time, exercise, and research.

1. **Reward:** Acknowledge hard work or the completion of an unpleasant task
2. **Stress buster:** Avoid something unpleasant by stepping away from life for a little while
3. **Alone or "me" time:** Dedicate time to focus on myself
4. **Exercise:** Walking around is better than sitting in front of the TV or the computer
5. **Research:** Observe the latest trends the retailers are focusing on

Any time I spent with a retailer and it fell into 1 of the 5 buckets, I did not allow myself to make a purchase. And if I did happen to cross the line and buy something, the very next day I would revisit the store and return the item—a penalty for not adhering to the reason why I was in the store.

Asking yourself upon arrival why you are in the store lets you set the ground rules for what your shopping experience should be. For a shopaholic, you may discover that often the purpose of your frequent visits to retailers was not because you needed to purchase something, it's because you wanted something and that something is an emotional payoff, not really more stuff for your wardrobe. Asking yourself "why am I here" brings your attention back to the point of shopping, to purchase goods. Over time I got really tired of asking myself "why" and I slowly stopped visiting retailers as often. Having to constantly put in extra work, when all I wanted to do was zone out and shop, took the fun out of shopping. And when shopping doesn't give you the same payoff that it used to, you aren't going to do it as often.

Hit The Brakes:
Practice shopping to retrain your brain

One of the hardest requests that you can ask a shopaholic to do is to stop shopping. Shopping is a task that can't be avoided forever—sooner or later, you are going to have to do it. Earlier in this chapter I said that there are 3 stages of shopping: browsing, stalking, and buying. Breaking the cycle of dependence on shopping required that I start small and then build upon these steps over time. Incorporating small changes allowed my brain chemistry to adjust slowly to my new behavior. I began with the first step, browsing. Browsing is the act of casually looking at something that is for sale. The key with browsing is that I am looking, and only looking, *not* buying something. I started with fine tuning my browsing skills because the first thing a shopper must do before finding an item to buy is browse to see what's for sale.

Focus on browsing

To work on my browsing prowess I began with online retailers. Online shopping provides both flexibility and privacy. I can click off of a retail site a lot faster than I can physically walk out of a store or a shopping mall. And if I want to write a list or use a timer while I browse in the comfort of my own home, no one ever has to know. I set a time limit for how long I could spend on the website and a goal for what I was trying to accomplish during that session. Locate a top for a new pair of pants? Select a little black dress, simply because I didn't own one yet? Identify a new pair of jeans in a style said to be the latest trend? Search for a black cardigan because all of my sweaters were pullovers? What I was shopping for didn't matter; what was important, was that I stayed focused on only that one goal during my shopping session, and that I adhered to the pre-set time. When the chime rang, the shopping session was over. If I had a saved credit card on the account, I deleted it to prevent any oops moments. More than once I would find myself reaching for my credit card during my browsing session. I kept a post-it note wrapped around my credit card with one question written on it, "do you *need* it?" If I was browsing then my answer is obviously going to be "no" and back into the wallet the credit card went.

For my earliest sessions, I used the timer on my phone set to 5 minutes, selected one retailer's website to browse, chose a goal for that session, and then just browsed. Any time I saw something that fit into my goal, I saved the item into the wishlist (or shopping cart if there was no wish list). When my session time was over, I simply logged out of the site. At first, I was logging multiple 5-minute sessions each day, visiting a new retailer each time, and saving at least 10 items during my visits. Originally, the clothes I selected did not always fit into the objective for my shopping session, I would veer off track. While perusing the dress selection I would suddenly stumble upon a blue and yellow print wrap dress that I just had to have, heedless of the fact that I was there to shop for a black one. No problem, I simply added it to the wishlist. I let myself freely browse until I began to browse with a purpose. After a short time, I could scan page after page looking for only the item that was the goal of my browsing session. Eventually I could pass over dresses in prints and colors that did not fit my criteria of black cocktail style. Then the day came when I really stepped up, and I began to use the search and find features on a retailer's website. Instead of merely browsing all of the options in a given category, I would limit the selection by inputting the criteria into the search fields. If I wanted a black cardigan, I simply set the color range to black and the style to cardigan and removed all other options. I no longer browsed all of the cardigans that were for sale, just the options that were indeed black. Not only did this speed up my shopping sessions, but it also helped me to stay on track by narrowing down the selection. And when I was able to browse without walking away feeling like I was missing out on something magical, I knew I was able to browse with a purpose and move on to the next step.

Focus on stalking

After selecting an item for purchase, a shopper has 2 options: run to the register and make the purchase, or put it back on the shelf and wait until the price drops. I always enjoy buying clothes when they are on sale. Do you?

For this step we are going to focus on fine-tuning your stalking skills. Pick an item that you want, then wait for the price to drop lower. The goal here is to wait, instead of buying something the minute you want it. The delay before purchasing breaks the rush of "I see it, I've got to have it immediately." Also, sometimes the long delay while waiting for a price to fall will be long enough that you may not even want the item by the time it goes on sale. That's exactly what happened to me.

I once stalked a three-quarter sleeve cashmere sweater for 3 months. The first time I saw it, I fell in love and I thought that I had to have that sweater. But it was expensive and I was over both my budget and my item limit for the month, so I left it on the shelf. Starting small, I decided to try out waiting on buying the sweater for 1 week. Every single day I looked at that sweater, and every day it was still in stock in my size. When the week ended I realized that I had survived the entire week without the new sweater that I originally just had to have. This made me curious about how long could I go until I purchased the sweater? I opted to check in on the sweater every single day. And every day I was able to get dressed with other pieces from my closet and the sweater stayed in stock in my size.

One day a few weeks later, the sweater went on sale for 40% off. I was thrilled, now it's time to buy! I waited all this time and it's finally on sale. But curiosity made me pause—I had survived without the sweater, this time for weeks, what if I went a little longer? Curious once again, I decided to track how long the sweater was on sale in my size. And 3 weeks later, it was still on sale. So I kept watching it. Finally, it was reduced even further, now 50% off! Well surely now must be the time to buy, right? But at that point it was 3 months since I first stalked the sweater and the cold weather season was going to be ending soon. I still liked the sweater, but after 3 months of dressing for cold weather without it, it was clear to me that I didn't need the sweater.

Focus on purchasing

After you have mastered browsing and stalking on the internet, without making a purchase, it's time to address the final step of shopping, the act of purchasing itself. For this step, it's time to up the ante and proceed into the lion's den itself, the brick and mortar stores, so that you may practice your new skills. Unlike online shopping, in-person shopping requires more time and more effort. It takes longer to physically walk away from a store when you have to do so in person. And it is twice as difficult to decide not to buy something when faced with the visual of only one left in your size on the racks. I was very nervous when I proceeded to this step, but I had already become skilled at the online stores, which gave me the confidence that the time had come for me to take the next step. As with the last 2 steps, you'll proceed the same as before, with pre-specified goals and time limits for your shopping sessions, but this time, I'm going to add in a few more tactics to help you out: chants and penalties.

A chant is a repeated phrase set to a melody and most commonly occurs when a group says a religious prayer or a slogan during a protest. For myself, I used the chant to help me stay focused on the task at hand during my in-person shopping sessions. The rhythmic nature of a chant made it more fun to say (and remember) than a bunch of plain words. I would design the chant prior to visiting the retailer, then I repeated the chant in my head (or out loud if I really needed to wake myself up) so that the reason why I was in the store, and not the appeal of new items, stayed at the forefront of my mind throughout my shopping visit.

My 2 favorite chants were:

1. I'm here for [insert emotional reason; for example, me time], not to buy
2. I'm looking for a [insert specifics of item here] and not [insert item that is tempting me]

Chant 1 was crafted before entering the store and remained the same throughout my shopping session. It helped to ground me as to the reason why I was in the store, from an emotional perspective. If I am shopping for any emotional reason, I am seeking a release of that emotion, not an actual good, therefore I should not be buying anything. Chant 1 forced me to recognize the times when I was shopping because I felt happy, sad, proud, scared, etc.

Chant 2 was designed based on the actual desired goods. Chant 2 was half created prior to entering a store, and it was not completed until after I was faced with temptation. The first half requires me to recognize what I am seeking to buy within the store (a black dress, a blue sweater, a brown pair of shoes, etc). The second half of Chant 2 is added when I ponder wanting to purchase something I stumbled upon during my searching. This portion is designed to redirect my attention so that I remain focused on what I am in the store to buy.

I began with chanting out loud in the car, before I even reached the parking lot of the store. And my first couple of visits I spent more time in the store chanting to myself, than I spent time actually reviewing what was on the sale racks. I was not used to reminding myself why I was in the store and it took all of my concentration to keep myself from wandering off track while I was inside. After a couple of months, I was able to walk around a store and only have to chant to myself when I picked up an item off of the shelf.

It had taken a while, but I eventually conditioned myself to walk in and out of the stores without any unneeded purchases. When this happened I finally realized that sometimes it's OK to visit and be "just looking." I don't have to buy something every single time, just because I am there. It is OK to walk out (or click off of the page) empty handed because my purpose for the visit wasn't to make a purchase.

Hit The Brakes:
Set item and budget limits for every month

The idea here is really straightforward: pick a number for how many items you want to buy, as well as how much money you want to spend, each month for 1 year. For example, 1 item with a budget of $250 each month. Over 1 year that would be 12 items at a cost of $3,000. The point of this strategy is that by setting item and budget limits, you'll shop with more focus, because you can only add a few things at a time.

If you try this strategy and find yourself struggling, going over your item and budget limits every month, then you probably didn't pick the right starting numbers for you. For this technique to work, you have to select a limit that you are comfortable with, and while I used 1 in the example, your starting number may be higher. It was for me. As someone who was used to buying a lot of stuff at one time, suddenly limiting myself to just 1 item per month was too drastic a change for me. The pressure to "pick just one" left me frustrated, I just couldn't pick one thing!

Instead, I limited myself to a dozen items for the first month, 8 the second, 6 the third, etc, slowly reducing the amount that I could buy over the course of 1 year. And I didn't stop with just how much I could buy, I also focused on limiting how much stuff I browsed for as well. Limiting the number of items that I focused on at one time helped me to really start paying attention to exactly what I wanted to buy: material, fit, style, design, color, laundry care, and the wardrobe capsule the item was for. Honing in on how carefully I analyzed a potential purchase helped me to write more targeted shopping lists for the times when I needed to add something to my wardrobe. It also helped me get over the notion that when I shopped I had to leave the store with a bag of stuff, sometimes it's OK to buy just 1.

Hit The Brakes:
Serve a penalty when you impulse purchase

In sports when a player breaks the rules, they are often given a penalty. Changing your shopping habits is no different. Despite a person's best attempts to improve, there may still be times that you might buy something when you didn't mean to. This happened to me often when I first started trying to change my shopping behavior. I said I was going to only buy 1 thing, and I walked away with 5, or I meant to just visit the store and browse and I walked out with a shopping bag. When your practice shopping sessions don't end the way that you planned, it's time to pay a penalty. In this case, you have 2 options: let go of it right away by returning what you bought, or give up something old for something new, by donating or discarding something from your closet so that the new addition has a place to go. No matter which option you choose, the point here is when you didn't do what you planned, you have to pay a price for your bad behavior.

At first, I found myself having to return clothes often. I'd buy something, go home, realize I didn't want to get rid of anything, and I'd have to go back to the store to make a return. When every new purchase put a bullseye on the stuff I already had, I started to think twice about what I was doing. After a while, having to return stuff almost every time I bought something became a deterrent, I didn't want to do returns anymore!

Hit The Brakes:
Find and participate in a support group or program

By nature, humans are social animals. We rely on each other to fulfill our hierarchy of needs. The hierarchy of needs for humans was first described by Abraham Maslow in his 1943 paper, "A Theory of Human Motivation."[9] The various needs for humans can be grouped into 5 categories:

1. Physiological (survival [breathing, food, water])
2. Safety (security [personal, financial, health])
3. Love/Belonging (friendship, family, intimacy)
4. Esteem (respect, confidence, status)
5. Self-actualization (creativity, problem solving, etc)

Parents or caretakers provide for these needs in infants. And as we age, we continue to rely on the participation and feedback of others; social interactions provide a primary opportunity for self-fulfillment. Support groups allow for connections with individuals who are in a similar situation and come in a variety of formats: internet, telephone, and in person.

Benefits of participating in support groups may include:

- Learn about resources and others' experiences

- Feel less alone or isolated

- Opportunity to talk about feelings and reduce stress and anxiety

- Develop a clearer understanding of the situation and options

9 Maslow AH. A theory of human motivation. *Psychological Review.* 1943;50(4):370-396.

- Gain a sense of control

- Hear about new/additional viewpoints

When I decided I no longer wanted to struggle by myself with overshopping, I joined a blog that I found on the internet. Through the blog community I received valuable advice and gained insights that I don't think I would have discovered on my own. I learned that I wasn't alone, there were other people out there who also had a shopping problem and were working hard on changing their behavior. And as I made progress in my own struggles, I felt comfortable enough to share my personal experiences to help others, eventually creating my own blog and writing this book.

To find a support group:
- Check the internet

- Ask a professional (counselor, psychiatrist, psychologist)

- Look at flyers (libraries, retailers, athletic clubs, restaurants, local businesses)

To help you get started, here are some of the support groups that I've discovered on the internet:
- Addictions.com-Shopping
  http://www.addictions.com/shopping/

- Daily Strength-Shopping Addiction
  https://www.dailystrength.org/group/shopping-addiction

- End Closet Chaos-Recovering Shopaholic Facebook Group
  https://www.facebook.com/recoveringshopaholicdotcom/
- Supportgroups.com
  http://shopping-addiction.supportgroups.com/
- The Shulman Center for Compulsive Theft, Spending, and Hoarding
  http://www.shopaholicsanonymous.org/
- Yahoo Groups-Shopping Addicts Only
  https://groups.yahoo.com/neo/groups/Shoppingaddictsonly/info

The world is filled with lots of people. The only way you are truly alone is if you choose not to reach out to others. In today's age of technological advancements there is no excuse for not finding a way to connect with someone. It might be awkward at first to lean on strangers for help, but once you realize that you are not alone, seeking comfort, support, and encouragement from other people in the same situation becomes a lot easier to do. There is strength in numbers. When a person is part of a group, if someone falls down, there is another person there to pick them up. And a little encouragement might be exactly what that person needs to help them get past their roadblocks.

Hit The Brakes:

Shop with a friend or relative who does not overshop

In a Canadian study[10] of more than 1,000 shoppers, people made more sensible decisions when shopping with a friend or a family member. Purchases were less likely to be impulsive and returned in the future. Overall, the study investigators noted that the emotional attachments that shoppers experienced were affected by the presence of a friend or relative. Together, confidence on purchasing decisions was increased. After all, a friend or relative will tell you if something truly looks good on you or not. And they will remind you of your shopping goals if you start to forget them.

I have experienced the positive benefits of shopping with a friend who is not an overshopper. A close friend and I visit our favorite store for their yearly sale, every year. For the past 8 years my friend and I have attended this sale, it has become our yearly ritual. We meet up for lunch, catch up on our lives, and then shop until we are ready to drop. And it is always great fun. One year during our day of shopping, I fell in love with a bright orange leather jacket. It fit me well, the color was very flattering, and I felt like a celebrity wearing it in the fitting

[10] Chebat J-C, Haj-Salem C, Oliveira S. Why shopping pals make malls different? *Journal of Retailing and Consumer Services.* 2014;21(2):77-85.

room. I really wanted this piece. But even at the sale price it was going to be a lot of money. My friend saw me start to waver from "oh this is lovely" to "oh I really want it" and that was her first red flag that something was amiss with my shopping decision. Then I began to put back everything else I was going to buy, just so I could purchase this out of my budget orange leather jacket. That was the second red flag for my friend.

Concerned by my behavior, my friend began to forcefully remind me that the sale price was indeed a great bargain, if the number one reason why I attended the sale was in search of an orange leather jacket. But that wasn't how I found the jacket. I stumbled across it while I browsed. I had never even considered that orange leather jackets existed, let alone want one for myself, prior to attending the sale. I was driven to purchase this jacket because I fell in love with it at first sight and it was an expensive item at a steep discount. Aghast that I would make a poor decision, my friend reminded me that I was considering purchasing a bright orange leather jacket, and she had never seen me wear the color orange, ever. Not even as a T-shirt. How could I consider buying a jacket of such high quality that it could last forever, in a color that I never wore? Did I really want to spend my money on this high-risk item?

I was annoyed that she was interfering with my purchase, and we started to argue. How dare she tell me how to spend my money? Doesn't she see how fabulous

I look in this jacket? It could become my new signature piece. As our tensions continued to rise, we eventually agreed that I would think about the jacket while we finished shopping the sale. If I still wanted it at the end of our visit, then I should purchase it. I asked the sales associate to hold the jacket while we shopped and spent the rest of my visit pondering whether or not to buy it. At the end of our shopping session I revisited the jacket. I realized that I still adored it, but it was not going to work for me, for all of the reasons my friend had stated earlier that day. Essentially, she was right. Years later, I still remember that jacket. And I am still happy that my friend helped me make the decision not to buy it.

Shopping with a friend or relative is a strategy that has helped to stop me from making a bad decision on what to buy, but it can also give the little extra nudge I needed to make a good purchase. While shopping for Christmas presents with DH, I mentioned that I really needed to replace my wool coat. Thinking that a new coat would make the perfect gift, we proceeded to the stores where I tried on coat, after coat, after coat, after coat. With a few hours of unsuccessful shopping under my belt, I was ready to give up on finding a new coat for my Christmas gift. Then DH saw it, a bright, banana yellow, wool coat. He asked me to try it on and I looked at him like he was crazy. I didn't think he had been paying attention the past few hours because all of the coats that I was looking at were neutral colors—black, gray, the occasional brown or ivory, but certainly no bright colors, especially yellow! To be a good sport I tried on the coat, and wouldn't you know, that crazy yellow color just worked on me. The coat wasn't too long or short, it had a zipper closure, and the bright yellow color enhanced my complexion. We purchased the coat, and for the next 7 years I wore that coat every winter. I never grew tired of the style or the color, and I always received compliments from strangers. When the coat developed a hole in the arm I continued to wear it. And when the lining ripped, I decided to wear my yellow coat for just 1 more year before finally retiring it.

Shopping with someone who is not an overshopper provides an opportunity to look at what you are thinking about buying with an alternative point of view. My shopping companion's viewpoints are different than my own, and they don't have any emotional attachments to the item that I am pondering. This allows my shopping buddy to be critical, rather than emotional, when reviewing my potential purchases.

Remaining critical about what you are doing when you go shopping is a key factor in helping to ensure that you buy something based on *need* and not *want*. Understanding *why* you went to the store, enlisting the help of friends, family members, and support groups, setting limits, holding yourself accountable by serving penalties when you veer off course, and practicing shopping all help you to remain aware of what you are doing when you shop. And when you are paying attention to your behavior when you shop, you lessen the influence of your neurotransmitters to drive you to buy something based on *want* instead of *need*. In doing so you lower the chance that you'll make an impulse purchase.

If you want to own a closet filled with clothes that you love and wear, then you have to take the necessary steps to ensure that when you buy something, you know what you are doing. You also need to make sure that you are keeping an eye on your wardrobe, otherwise it can start to increase in size without you knowing about it.

Chapter 7 recap:

If you want to shop successfully you'll have to work at it.

Hit The Brakes:
Before you shop ask yourself "why am I here?"

- When you enter a store, question why you are there to find out if you're shopping because you *need* it or because you *want* it

Hit The Brakes:
Practice shopping to retrain your brain

- To practice how to look for something without getting side tracked, select a time limit, online retailer, and goal for what you are searching for, then browse until time is up

- Pick an item that you want, then stalk it—wait to buy until the price drops lower—to curb the need to buy it as soon as you find it

- Write and repeat chants while you are in a brick and mortar store to help you stay focused on why you are there so that you become accustomed to leaving a store with only 1 new purchase, or none

Hit The Brakes:
Set item and budget limits for every month

- Choose how many to add and how much to spend for each month over 1 year to focus your attention on what you are buying. If you struggle to start with 1 item per month, go higher, then reduce the number over time

Hit The Brakes:
Serve a penalty when you impulse purchase

- Make yourself return or donate unplanned things that you bought as a way to curb bad behavior

Hit The Brakes:
**Find and participate in a support group
or program**

- If you struggle with a shopping addiction, remember that you are not alone. Joining a group of people who understand and struggle with the same issues might offer you encouragement and support when you need it

Hit The Brakes:
**Shop with a friend or relative who does
not overshop**

- Ask a friend or relative to go shopping with you so that they can help you avoid making bad decisions and encourage you to make good ones when you want to buy something

Learning to shop with a purpose, instead of shopping just because you feel like it, is one way to ensure that you will buy things that you need instead of just more stuff that you want.

Chapter 8

Preventive wardrobe maintenance

Catch anything serious before
it becomes a major problem

Did anyone ever tell you that owning a wardrobe is sometimes similar to owning a car? Don't believe me? Consider this. A regular service schedule, including oil changes, checking air pressure in tires, replacing filters, belts, hoses, etc, can help your car continue to run its best. Cars that haven't undergone preventive maintenance run a high risk of breaking down, require more expensive repairs, and often have a shorter life span. Your wardrobe requires a similar level of care, and you are responsible for doing the work. Maintaining your wardrobe requires that you pay attention to 2 areas: 1) what you are keeping in your closet and 2) what you are bringing into your closet. To help you manage your wardrobe, this chapter covers tips you may want to keep in mind so that your wardrobe will always contain all of the things that you need, and none of the things that you don't. Let's begin with the closet itself.

Hit The Brakes:
Be mindful of what you decide to KEEP inside your wardrobe

Wardrobe creep is the gradual act of adding more, and more, and more clothes, with the new additions ultimately taking over the wardrobe. Wardrobe creep often starts small and is almost unnoticeable. It begins when a single new garment is added, without one being permanently removed. The addition of something new, without the removal of something old, is failing to adhere to the one in/one out rule discussed in Chapter 4 during The DH Closet Challenge. As a wardrobe increases in size, the closet becomes cluttered and its performance declines. Outfit combinations that once worked well become buried among layers of new clothes, leaving you struggling to find something to wear. I've identified 5 ways to help you maintain the size of your closet, starting with the tip I've talked about the most throughout this book.

Closet Maintenance #1—
One in/one out your purchases

When your closet is at a size that works well for you, the only way to keep it that way is to make sure that every time you add something, you also remove something, ie, one in/one out your purchases. Every time I haven't done this in the past, my wardrobe has quickly crept up in size. This became particularly apparent with my shoe capsule when I participated in The DH Closet Challenge. During the challenge I didn't include my shoes, only my clothes. Big mistake. Just how fast did my shoe capsule grow in size? When I started The DH Closet Challenge I owned 19 pairs of shoes. During the challenge I bought 10 new pairs of shoes at one time. My shoe capsule went from 19 pairs of shoes to 29 pairs of shoes, an increase of 53%!

In an attempt to be conscientious of how quickly I was adding to my shoe wardrobe, I returned 3 bad purchases before I even left the mall. That left me arriving at home with 7 new pairs of shoes instead of 10, a 37% increase. Once I arrived at home, I selected an additional 3 pairs of shoes to donate. Ten original purchases minus 6 total returned/donated pairs, left an increase of only 4 pairs of shoes to my shoe wardrobe. Yet despite my best efforts, the size of my shoe wardrobe still went from 19 to 23 pairs of shoes, a 21% increase at one time.

Sure, through returns and donations, I was able to add less shoes to my closet than what I originally bought, but I still added new shoes without removing an equal amount of old shoes.

Any increase, no matter how small, is still an increase.

The addition of 4 new pairs of shoes meant that my shoe wardrobe experienced wardrobe creep. An increase of only 4 pairs of shoes doesn't sound like a whole lot, but if you constantly add new stuff, eventually your wardrobe will double or even triple in size. And that's why following the one in/one out rule is so important to keep your wardrobe at a consistent size over the long term.

An additional benefit to practicing one in/one out for the things that you buy is that it forces you to be accountable for the items within your wardrobe. When buying something new brings with it the penalty of having to remove something old, it might make you pause and reconsider your purchase. I know it always does for me. I end up asking myself, "do I *really* need the new item?" And if my answer is "yes" the follow-up question is, "what old item will be removed to make room for the new one?" Many times I ask myself these 2 questions and end up walking out of the store without buying anything, because I don't have something at home that I want to remove from my wardrobe.

Following the one in/one out rule shouldn't just be triggered upon the purchase of something new. You'll also want to do this when there is a shift of function for the clothes already within your wardrobe. For example, sometimes I downgrade my wardrobe items. A nice sweater that was once worn to work, gets relegated to function as a cozy house sweater for lounging around before it is donated or thrown out. When I do this, I must remain conscientious about the input/output flow of the items in my closet. Yes, it is fine to downgrade a sweater;

however, for every sweater that I downgrade from the function of a nice sweater that was worn to work to a comfy house sweater that is worn for lounging around, I must remember that 1 older sweater that was serving the function of lounging at home now has to go. If I don't manage the flow, I'll end up clogging up my loungewear capsule, and suddenly own a rather large accumulation of not-so-nice sweaters that I don't feel great wearing. Therefore, for every sweater that I downgrade, one now has to go.

Closet maintenance #2—
Perform regular closet evaluations and editing

Nothing in life remains static, and that includes lifestyle needs and fashion preferences. One season you might be interested in sporting a wardrobe filled with blues and greens, and the next season a wardrobe of only white and black. Garments may routinely be passed over because the item no longer fits your current size, the materials have become worn out or damaged, or it simply no longer fits into your style preferences. A wardrobe that functions well is in a constant state of flux. Adding in new things at the same rate as you take out the old is one way to keep your closet moving forward.

Another way you can keep your closet from growing stagnant over time is to carve out dedicated time to analyze your closet. When you use the tips discussed in Chapter 2 to assess not only what you still have inside, but also examine how often you're using the item, you can spot when something you own has fallen out of favor. And when you know what you own, you'll also notice when a specific type of garment has increased in number. For example, if I routinely add white T-shirts, after a while I'm going to have removed all of my old T-shirts and be left with only white ones. If I don't take a minute to pause and recognize that I own a bunch of white T-shirts already, I'll just keep blindly adding more, thinking that I still need them. It doesn't matter if you prefer to edit your closet all at once with one long session or often with shorter (quarterly, monthly, or even weekly) sessions, for a closet to remain up to date and fully functional, sooner or later you'll want to set aside some time to reassess what is in your wardrobe.

Closet maintenance #3—
Limit wardrobe repeats

One of the downfalls with owning a large number of the same type of item is that you might start to believe that you *have* to own a lot of it. Remember my collection of 30 sweaters that I mentioned back in Chapter 2? I had sweaters that were the same color but different styles, and sweaters that were the same style but different colors. How did I end up with so many? What I realize today is that there were 3 reasons why my sweater collection grew out of control: 1) I clearly wasn't following the one in/one out rule when I added to my closet, 2) I obviously wasn't taking the time to review what I already had in my closet, and 3) when I went shopping, I always looked at and bought sweaters. In the stores I would often remember that I owned a lot of sweaters, but I would not always be able to recall all of the colors or the styles that I owned. Instead of viewing my large sweater collection as something that required an evaluation and editing session, I interpreted my large sweater collection as proof that I needed sweaters. After all, I owned a lot of them, so surely I must use them and should shop for more, right? And shop I would, and ultimately I would buy yet another sweater.

Owning lots of sweaters brought with it another downfall. Should I wear all of them once before repeating again or should I simply select my favorites and repeat wearing those as often as possible? If I wanted to actually use all of my sweaters, I would have to wear 1 every single day. Which means that I wouldn't be able to sport any other toppers, including blazers, vests, ponchos, etc for the entire month. The sweater colors and styles would probably change over the 30 days, but I'd still be wearing yet another sweater. And that often led me to grow bored with my wardrobe. But, if I select a handful of sweaters that I really like and repeatedly wear, leaving the rest untouched, I'll never use everything I own, and unused clothing is wasted money.

To prevent yourself from getting bored with your wardrobe, limit the number of repeats you keep in your closet. If you aren't sure how many is too many, you can run a mini version of The DH Closet Challenge from Chapter 4. Simply select the same type of item every single day until you get bored and reach for something else. The number of days you can go before you change will give you a jumping off point with how many to own of something. For example, I sported 1 sweater from my collection every day. After 4 days I grew bored of wearing sweaters and reached for a blazer. On the sixth day I grabbed a cardigan, and on the seventh day I once again reached for a sweater. Over 1 week I used 5 sweaters. This doesn't mean that I have to immediately toss the remaining 25 sweaters, but the results of this mini version of The DH Closet Challenge suggest that I may not need as many sweaters as I own, since I couldn't even go 1 week wearing them every single day. With this knowledge I can now work to reduce the total number of sweaters I have over time. If you find that you go past 1 week, simply extend the challenge until you finally do reach for another type of item.

What do you do if you find yourself suddenly owning a lot of one item and you want to pare it down a little? Using the shoe wardrobe I mentioned at the beginning of this chapter, I'm going to present you with 3 options you may want to try:

1. Reduce the number of items in the largest categories. In my shoe wardrobe, I owned the most shoes for my spring and fall capsules. Out of 23 pairs

of shoes, spring and fall combined contained 11 pairs. If I limited the total number of shoes for spring and fall to 4 pairs, 2 for spring and 2 for fall, I can remove 7 pairs of shoes, decreasing the size of my shoe wardrobe by roughly 30%.

2. Select only 1 core color across categories. If I saved only my black shoes (I have 9 pairs of them), I can drastically reduce the number of shoes that I own once again; this time I can remove 14 pairs of shoes, decreasing the size of my shoe wardrobe by 61%.

3. Choose only 1 style across categories. I sometimes purchase the same style of shoe in 2 (or more) different colors. For example, I have tall boots in both black and brown, ballet flats in black, nude, and turquoise, and sandals in black and turquoise. If I only kept 1 of each style, I could remove 4 pairs of shoes, decreasing my shoe wardrobe by 17%.

It doesn't matter if the repeat stems from owning more than 1 of the same style or of the same color, the excessive repetition is why a wardrobe might creep up over time. Eliminating the repeats in your wardrobe can greatly reduce the total number of items that you own.

Closet maintenance #4—
Save the memory not the item

One of the biggest reasons why stuff is given a free pass from adhering to the one in/one out rule is when the clothes have sentimental value. T-shirts from a concert, the gown from your wedding, a scarf from a dream vacation, all of these pieces are from once-in-a-lifetime events and are irreplaceable. These mementos are physical connections to something you did in the past and have the potential to be passed on, so you hold on to them. I've done this a lot, after all, surely I can pass down these items to family members or perhaps someone that I know will want these precious pieces of mine once I'm gone? Right? Maybe or maybe not.

Unfortunately, there is no guarantee that an item that was special to me will also be cherished or desired by someone else. As I continue to age, and the special events in my life rise in number, I require more space to store these mementos. And if I am fortunate to live to an old age, I'll eventually run out of closet space for all of my special things. When all of my closets are stuffed full of items I don't use, this takes away valuable storage space for the things that I do use. Now I'm not saying to get rid of everything that has sentimental value, but I do encourage you to consider how many sentimental pieces of clothing you own, and how much storage space it takes up. If you own more things that you are not using, than you are using, it may be time to consider a different strategy.

When the number of special things is too high, or you've simply run out of room, save a picture instead. Pictures of garments are easier to store, and can still provide the function of serving as a physical reminder of the past event, thus helping to spark a memory of a special occasion. Pictures are also easier to transport and can be duplicated. And pictures can be displayed outside of a closet. I can take a picture of my wedding dress and frame it for my desk, tack it up to a memory board in my closet, or provide a copy to my sister to serve as a reference when she shops for her own dress. But if I only have the dress itself, I am unable to disperse the information as easily. By saving the memory and not the item itself, I am able to stop wardrobe creep due to special occasion items.

Closet maintenance #5—
Use everything you own

Another reason why stuff is given a free pass from adhering to the one in/one out rule, is when your lifestyle needs have changed. A new job, pregnancy, weight gain, weight loss, retirement, starting a new hobby, stopping an old hobby, these are all examples of the circumstances that can affect the functionality of a wardrobe. Sometimes the change in a person's life is short lived; for example, I could join a gym one month, and by the next, I may have already lost interest. Other times, the lifestyle change lasts a little longer; for example, pregnancy runs an average of 9 months for most women, and typically at some point in this process, maternity clothing is required. As life presses onward and clothing requirements continue to change, it becomes easy to want to hold on to older clothes. If the gym membership was put on hold due to injury, I'm not going to want to throw away all of my workout clothing right away. The same logic holds true for pregnancy; most pregnant woman anticipate fitting back into their pre-pregnancy clothing after giving birth. This uncertainty about the future allows unused garments to remain in a wardrobe. This practice leaves a closet highly susceptible to wardrobe creep, leading to a decline in its ability to support your dressing needs.

**A functional closet stores the clothes
that let you build outfits,
not a bunch of random items that you can't use.**

Once again using my shoe wardrobe as the example, the reason why I failed to adhere to one in/one out for my shoes was because I couldn't decide which of my older shoes were necessary to keep for my current lifestyle, if any. Instead of forcing myself to face the reality that I was shopping for new shoes because my old shoes were no longer working, I opted to simply ignore that I owned shoes I was not using. Instead I kept my attention on the shoes in my closet that I was using.

When I realized what I was doing, I had to come up with an action plan for how to streamline my shoe wardrobe. Too often, I had the habit of saving a new purchase for a later date. Does this sound familiar? A high-heeled shoe that would be great for an occasion that hasn't even come up yet, or a wedge heel that would be fantastic with the "right" ensemble, or a day of perfect weather to sport a block heel boot for the first time with flare jeans. To keep from saving my stuff I ran a simple experiment—set aside enough time to wear every pair of shoes I owned once, and then did just that. For 3 weeks I wore a new pair of shoes every single day. Fancy high-heeled special occasion shoes with jeans and a blazer to dress them down, boots with flare jeans, etc. The goal here is to assess 2 things: 1) are the shoes I've been saving actually comfortable enough to wear and 2) do I really want to wear the shoes?

Keeping a close eye on how often I am, or am not, using an item in my wardrobe, in this case shoes, allows me to make sure that no pieces get left behind and go unused for a long period of time. If I allow myself to add new items to my wardrobe, but I don't begin to regularly use the item, I'm left with wasted money and clutter in my closet.

How often each pair of shoes (or any item in your closet) should be worn to maintain a place in your wardrobe is a personal decision. One person may want to wear all of their things once a week, and someone else, once a season. If you are waiting to lose weight, gain weight, bounce back from a pregnancy, or heal from an injury it could take months before you can assess some of the clothes in your wardrobe. With no right or wrong answer here, it's up to you to decide how long is too long, keeping in mind, the longer something sits unworn in your closet, the less chance that you will start wearing it again.

If you aren't sure what you need inside your wardrobe and you find yourself struggling to use everything that you own, you may want to review one of the closet challenges discussed in Chapter 4.

Hit The Brakes:
Be mindful of what you decide to
ADD to your wardrobe

Keeping a close eye on what's inside your wardrobe at all times helps prevent your wardrobe from spiraling out of control because it increased in size. Just as important is making sure that the things you add to your closet you'll actually be able to use. You may want to keep in mind the following 4 tips when you shop to help keep the size of your wardrobe small and the frequency that you use your clothes high.

Shopping maintenance #1—
Buy stuff you can use today

If this tip sounds familiar, that's because I first mentioned it back in Chapter 3 as it can be used to guide you on what to get rid of when you clean out your closet. This tip is also good to keep in mind when you are shopping for something new. If you want to use everything that you own (or come pretty close to using it all anyway) you'll have to make sure that you purchase and own stuff that you can actually use. Spending money on clothing you hope to use one day in the future, but can't use today, takes away money and storage space for something you can enjoy today instead. And the more clothes in your closet you have that you can't use, the more you'll want (and need) to shop and buy new things so you own something you actually can use.

**Shopping maintenance #2—
Purchase multi-use/function items**

Special events can easily increase the size of a wardrobe. An invitation to a wedding, bridal shower, birthday party, a request to attend a job interview, or even taking a vacation are not everyday occurrences, and these special events often provide the opportunity to shop for something new. And often I do. My day-to-day lifestyle does not require clothing for any of these special occasions and it is always fun for me to attend a lifetime event in a new outfit. However, a dress purchased for a formal wedding that continues to sit unworn in the closet for months and ultimately years afterwards, leaves the garment with a really high cost per wear. A wiser course of action would be to purchase clothes that can be used for multiple occasions. But is this really possible? Every single time, no of course not. I'm not going to be able to wear a gown for a formal wedding to my current job, and I'm certainly not going to sport it on the weekends running errands either. But there are times when clothes can be multi-functional.

For example, one time, DH and I took a week-long holiday to a Caribbean island. We stayed at a resort with both daytime and evening dress codes and had plans to spend large amounts of time participating in the watersports that were available. The daytime dress codes were easy, I already owned plenty of shorts and T-shirts. However, the watersports and the evening dress codes were another matter. I did not own anything suitable in my existing wardrobe, not in the working closet or among the items in the boutique (items that were on hold during The DH Closet Challenge). This meant that I had to shop!

At first, I wanted to purchase 7 new outfits for the watersports activities, 1 for each day of the vacation. Fortunately, I was in the middle of The DH Closet Challenge at the time, and I had already become comfortable owning a smaller wardrobe. I did not want to vastly expand my vacation capsule within my existing wardrobe just for our upcoming holiday. DH and I do not always spend our holidays at beach locations, nor do we often participate in watersports. This past behavior means that the items I would purchase, whose use was specific for only a beach holiday, could potentially sit unworn for a year or longer once the holiday was over.

Ultimately, I purchased only 1 new outfit for the watersport activities, and I ensured that this outfit could be layered over my existing collection of swimsuits. I also made sure that I selected an outfit with material that would dry quickly so that I could reuse the outfit every day. In doing so, after the holiday was over, I would only be left with 1 watersport outfit sitting in the vacation capsule within my wardrobe, instead of an entire week's worth of outfits. And since the watersport outfit was meant to be worn over a swimsuit, I opted to use the watersport outfit as my beach cover-up, thus eliminating the need to purchase an additional cover-up for my swimsuits.

The wardrobe hole of beach vacation evening wear was a little more challenging. At the time, I was not a big dress gal and I would rarely sport a dress during my day-to-day lifestyle. With these factors in mind, I had to pay close attention to both the number and the style of the dresses I was adding to my wardrobe. As a non-dress gal, an addition of 7 nights' worth of dresses would be a very large increase to my wardrobe, and runs a very high risk of sitting unworn after the beach vacation.

Instead of purchasing 7 dresses, one for each night, I opted to add only 4. With an 8-day, 7-night vacation, I would be able to wear each dress twice during the holiday. By rotating the dresses, I still had variety for the week, but I was hopefully not going to overload my wardrobe with dresses that I may never wear again.

The style of the dresses was especially important for my beach vacation capsule. I wanted to ensure that these new purchases would be used *after* the beach vacation. The stores were flooded with maxi dresses, tank top or racerback style dresses, and loose chiffon options, and none of these were appropriate for my work environment. Since I work 5 out of 7 days per week, this meant that any dresses that were not suitable for work would sit unworn for the majority of the workweek. Additionally, many of the dress options featured short or no sleeves, neither of which would keep me warm in air-conditioned settings, which is where I spend most of my time during the warm weather months. The stores contained plenty of dress options perfect for a beach vacation, but not ideal for use in my day-to-day lifestyle.

Ultimately, I purchased 4 dresses for my beach vacation that would also be appropriate for my daily life. The garments were made with lightweight materials and contained neutral prints and colors. When making my selections, I paid close attention to the style of the dress itself, ensuring that only those dresses that would layer well with the cardigans and blazers from my business capsule were added to my wardrobe. The classic patterns, structures, colors, and materials of my new dresses worked well for the beach holiday, layered with fun jewelry and footwear, and also functioned nicely in my business capsule when paired with more classic toppers and shoes. Keeping in mind the long-term potential use, and not just the immediate use, of my new dresses ensured I was able to use these pieces more often than just on a beach holiday.

One of my favorite tricks is to use accessories and a change of shoes to increase the functionality of a garment. A black lace dress worn with heels for a wedding can be paired with a denim jacket and ballet flats for a cute date night look. A pair of chinos and a white tank top that were worn with flip flops on a beach holiday can be paired with wedge sandals and a blazer for a casual office environment. If you receive an invitation to a special event, or you are going on a vacation to somewhere that requires special clothing, you may want to keep in mind if you'll be able to use the garment in one of your day-to-day wardrobe capsules.

Shopping maintenance #3—
Stick to existing core/base colors

A wardrobe that is left unchecked can quickly begin to house wardrobe orphans. Back in Chapter 3, one of the tips to help you clean out your closet was to pick one core color. This tip is also great to keep in mind when shopping for something new. Only adding clothes that will pair with your chosen core color will help to keep a wardrobe capsule small in size. I also keep this tip in mind when I'm packing for a trip. This tip keeps popping up in this book because more colors don't always lead to more outfits. Often, it's the exact opposite. More colors lead to *less* outfit combinations, and typically end up requiring many additional items to create the look. An outfit with a black top and white jeans may look lovely paired with black footwear, but swap out the black top for yellow, and now the black footwear no longer looks best, a nude option might be preferred instead. Keep the yellow top, but swap out the white jeans for a brown trouser, and now a brown shoe will be required to complete the look. You don't have to own a wardrobe filled with only 1, 2, or 3 colors, but when it comes to your smaller wardrobe capsules, owning less colors will help to keep the total number of items small while ensuring everything inside can be mixed and matched easily.

For example, one of the smaller capsules in my wardrobe is for business meetings. I don't have many occasions for business attire within a year, so I use a core neutral color of black to maintain a smaller size for this wardrobe capsule. I don't purchase anything for this wardrobe capsule that does not pair well with black. I have a black suit, a black pair of shoes and boots, a black tote, and a few blouses with prints that all contain black in them. By sticking to one core color, I am able to mix and match within this capsule to create additional outfits. The blazer of the black suit can be worn with any of the blouses because they all have black in the print. I do not need to purchase additional colors of shoes, because all of the items in this capsule pair well with black footwear. And I do not require more than one work tote, again because everything pairs well with black.

When I shop for new additions for this capsule, I look for colors and prints that will pair well with black.

By focusing my purchases around one core color I am able to quickly narrow down potential items. When I am shopping I don't become side tracked or overwhelmed by pretty colors and prints that will require purchasing additional items to create an outfit. It is easy for me to maintain a business capsule with lots of remixing potential for outfits despite its smaller size.

I apply the same concept when packing for a trip. I select one core neutral. Once again, I'll use black. For a trip to a cold location I may pack black jeans, black trousers, black boots and black sweaters. I'll toss in 1 or 2 colored tops and jackets to add a little interest to my outfits. But by sticking to a core of black, I am able to limit my shoe options to only black footwear. Now, instead of having to pack multiple colored shoes that may only work with 1 or 2 outfits, I can pack the same color of footwear, in multiple styles: flat boots, heeled boots, ballet flats, sneakers, etc.

Over the years I have learned that, for some mystery reason, footwear that is 100% comfortable and blister free at home, suddenly becomes less comfortable and prone to leaving blisters on a trip. This means that carrying a variety of footwear options is very important for me when I am away from home (and my closet). By selecting the core of black, if my feet are sore one day, it's not a problem, I can simply swap the footwear and still be able to sport any of the outfits I brought with me. But if I had packed outfits requiring multiple colored footwear, I most likely would not have also packed multiple styles of footwear, and I run the risk of not being able to use all of the clothing I brought for my trip.

Owning a wardrobe focused on variety through styles, and not colors alone, allows me to remix items more often, and to pack without worrying that an outfit will not function during a trip. A wardrobe has less of a chance to creep up in size if the core color number remains low.

Shopping maintenance #4—
Wear it before you duplicate it

Before you duplicate something make sure you've worn it first. Why? Sometimes, it looks like a good idea to buy 2 at one time, especially when the item in question has been difficult to find or fit, but you don't really know if you should duplicate the item or not, until you actually wear it. For example, shoes that fit my fussy feet are always a challenge for me. During one of my shopping trips, I stumbled upon a pair of gray round toe wedge shoes that I opted to add as my new shoe to my spring/summer wardrobe capsule. I thought the shoes were perfect. The wedge provided height, without the hassle of a heel, as well as stability. The design of the toe box easily accommodated my wider foot. And most important of all, they were comfortable. When I decided to purchase the gray version, I noticed that the shoes also came in a nude color. Now I've wanted a nude color shoe for a long time but always found a reason not to purchase them.

The heel was too high, the material was patent (patent doesn't accommodate my swelling feet), the nude color was not nude against my skin tone, or the shoe just didn't seem to fit properly on my foot. So when I saw that my new gray shoe came in my long wished for nude color, and was available in my size, I wanted to pounce on them.

Before I grabbed the nude color wedge and added it to my purchase, I realized that I had one little problem. Shoes are one of my hard to fit items. And in the past, I've owned shoes that were perfectly comfortable in the store, yet vastly uncomfortable once I tried to put them through the paces of my day-to-day life. This prior experience made me pause—how could I decide to immediately duplicate my new gray shoes when I had not put them to the test yet? Instead of pouncing on the second pair, I reluctantly left with only the gray shoes. Thank goodness I did. When I wore the gray shoes for a full day, I immediately realized that they were not 8-hour shoes. I often have the problem that my feet swell during the day and when a shoe exposes a lot of the top of the foot, it cuts into the skin above my big toe. And the gray wedge shoes were no different.

If I had immediately bought the nude color shoes, before I wore the gray pair, I would have ended up adding 2 pairs of sitting shoes to my wardrobe, which is not what I needed. I want my elusive nude color shoe to be an 8-hour shoe that I can wear often, not just on special occasions when I will be sitting a lot. Purchasing a nude color shoe in the style of the gray wedge would have been a poor purchasing decision.

When you are tempted to duplicate something in your wardrobe, ask yourself if you have worn the original first. If your answer is no, wait and wear it before you duplicate it. Sometimes you'll discover that your new wardrobe addition isn't going to work out as well as you originally planned, but you didn't know until you actually tried it out first.

Up to this point in this book you've been working on customizing your wardrobe so that it is the right wardrobe for you, and only you. Everything that you own is what you like, you can and do wear, and reflects your personal style. But sometimes despite one's attempts to the contrary, something sneaks into your wardrobe anyway. Other times, you just make a mistake, especially if you're someone who has been working hard on changing a bad habit that you've had for a long time. As an ex-shopaholic running into roadblocks happened to me all the time before I finally changed my behavior. In the next chapter I'm going to explain why we sometimes make a mistake with our wardrobe, and what you can do to prevent it from happening again in the future.

Chapter 8 recap:

Always keep one eye on what's inside your closet.

 Hit The Brakes:
Be mindful of what you decide to KEEP inside your wardrobe

- Every time you add something into your closet, decide what you are going to remove to keep your wardrobe at its current size

- Schedule time to review and edit your closet (daily, weekly, monthly, biannually, annually, etc) to spot either when you are no longer using something or when a specific type of garment has increased in number unintentionally

- Own less of the same type of item to avoid growing bored with your wardrobe

- Take a picture of an item to serve as a physical reminder of the special moment when you start to run out of storage space

- Pick something new to wear every day until you've worn everything that you own. Anything that fits your current body and lifestyle but you don't want to wear is a prime target that you may want to remove from your wardrobe

Hit The Brakes:

Be mindful of what you decide to ADD to your wardrobe

- Spend your money buying stuff you can use today, not on things you have to save for later, to keep your wardrobe small and functional

- Keep the long-term potential use, and not just the immediate use, of a new purchase top of mind to ensure that the clothes you buy can be used for more than one occasion

- Buy only the clothes that will pair with your chosen core color to keep a specific wardrobe capsule (or your entire wardrobe) small in number and able to mix and match easier

- Before duplicating, wear the first one to make sure that the item fits well and is comfortable

A wardrobe that is functioning well is able to keep up with the dressing needs of your current lifestyle. As demands change over time, keep a close eye on what you decide to keep, as well as what you add in to your closet. This will help your wardrobe keep up with changing times.

Chapter 9

Getting back on the wagon after falling off

One can often learn more from failure than from success

When someone relapses, they often think one thing—I have failed. I tried to make a change, but I slipped and fell back into my old ways. My attempts to do something different, to be someone different, were useless. I'm doomed to make the same mistakes over, and over, and over again. It doesn't matter if my behavior is due to a bad habit or an addiction, I'm going to be stuck this way—out of control—forever. But is a relapse really always a bad thing? After all, a person can't slip back into old behavior unless they've managed to move forward, making at least a little progress first. The problem wasn't that the bad habit or addiction couldn't be changed, the issue is that the change didn't last for the long term.

For example, when I worked to conquer my addiction to shopping, for a while I made great progress. I managed to reduce the size of my wardrobe, loved more of the clothes that I owned, dressed faster in the mornings, and spent my days pleased with my outfits. Then one day, standing inside my closet it felt like I had woken up from out of a trance. I looked around and I was crushed. My closet rod was once again stuffed to the point of breaking, my shelves had returned to their prior state of overflowing, and once more I was clueless on what to put together for an outfit when I dressed in the mornings. In my quest to master my wardrobe and change my behavior I had climbed halfway up to the top, slipped, and immediately tumbled all the way back to the bottom floor. I had suffered a relapse, and it made me feel hopeless.

As I mentioned in Chapter 1, an addiction to shopping doesn't always begin with a grandiose "aha" moment, sometimes the signs are subtle and the problem increases over time. And if bad habits and addiction don't develop overnight, then neither will making a change. The road to recovery is not a straight line for everyone. Sometimes it zigs and zags, filled with both highs and lows, success and disappointment. Relapses can and often do happen when someone is working towards overcoming an addiction. Relapses may be common, but they don't also have to be a setback. You can use a relapse as a marker to help keep you moving forward.

A relapse is an opportunity to learn.

The key to making a change last for the long haul is to be prepared, so that you can halt the descent as soon as it starts. A relapse is a sign that you've encountered a trigger, and that trigger caused you to slide backwards. Knowing what triggers you to shop and having a plan to halt the impulse before you can act is how you can keep your progress moving forward towards your end goal.

One of the many challenges for someone working on overcoming a shopping problem is that the act of shopping for clothes is seen as nothing out of the ordinary in today's society. The encouragement to shop and the praise for having bought something is everywhere. When I tell a friend or co-worker that I bought new clothes, this activity is not perceived as a bad thing to do. In fact, telling someone that I not only bought something new, but also how much I saved, is often met with high praise. "I saved $50 on this sweater." "I got 15% off these new boots." "Everything I bought was half off." The higher the savings, the greater the success. Not only is shopping for, and saving money on, clothes encouraged by family members, friends, and co-workers, but there's also an entire field of professionals dedicated to encouraging you to buy—the marketing industry. These professionals are focused on the answers to 2 key questions: 1) what is the customer's bullseye, ie, the emotional payoff the customer is looking for (to fit in, to stand out, etc), and 2) how can I hit the bullseye over, and over, and over again?

Collecting the information to answer these 2 questions is surprisingly easy. Most of today's retail stores have some type of rewards-based system. It may be a frequent shopper's card that is used at a grocery or drug store to save a few dollars on a purchase. It could be a store credit card that has designated shopper's days and members only savings days. Sometimes it's simply a matter of letting a web browser or social media network track your surfing habits, so that the ads on the screen start to mimic your interests or "likes." The longer you surf the web, the more information the tracking program can gather, thus allowing the ads to become specialized to target your likes and dislikes. Regardless of the source, the final goal is the same—figure out what that individual likes the most, and then present more opportunities to "save." Every time a retailer provides me the customer with an opportunity to "save," they are really presenting a chance for me to *spend*. The more chances I am given to spend, the higher the probability that I will. After all, a person can only say no to temptation so many times before they finally say yes.

Often when I visit a store, I'm asked to provide some type of personal information during my transaction. A phone number, an email address, a zip code, or maybe even all of these things. And this request is often, but not always, presented with a golden carrot. If I give my personal information, I'll be able to save money on my purchase, either the same day, at a later date, or both. Wanting to save money, I would tell the store everything, receive my savings offer, and walk out feeling like a million bucks. But giving away my personal information came with a price. The savings offers never stopped. This is because the next day, or perhaps a few days later, the marketers will step in. I receive a text message with a reward offer to return to the retailer to save money. I'm given a coupon at the time of purchase to fill out a survey for the store, just a couple of questions, and I can have 20% off savings on my next visit. I might receive daily emails highlighting a specific offering for each day. The incentives to *save, save, save,* if I just *spend, spend, spend,* will continue to roll on in—indefinitely. At first I thought I was the winner in this little game between the consumer and the marketer. "Look I saved 20% because I filled out that survey." But in reality, it was the marketers who were winning. This is because in order for me to receive a savings on my purchase, I have to return to the retailer and buy something!

Providing an opportunity to save is not the only way marketers trigger an impulse to shop. As time passes, the savings offer itself will change too. I'll receive a weekly email and the savings percentage will bounce around, one day it's 20%, the next day 30%, then 20% again, and then maybe a week later an elusive 40%. The low-high-low ploy works very well. If I see an offer going up and down, and up and down, and then suddenly I see a new number, I'm going to want to shop. After all, I haven't seen that 40% in a long time, so clearly now that everything is 40% it's the time to shop. When the savings offer rises to its highest I'd be off to the store.

Another form of ammunition the marketers use is customer reviews and recommendations. While I'm filling up my online shopping bag, I'll see a scrolling list of items "other customers interested in what I want also purchased" pop up on my screen. Curious what others who think like me were interested in, I'll look at their selections too. Or I'll receive an email from a retailer stating "you've purchased this item in the past and now this similar item is also available." Well I liked the old item, so I'll probably like the new version as well, and I'd grab that too.

When you shop as frequently as I have, you begin to notice the marketing strategies aimed at prompting a consumer to *buy, buy, buy.* They filter down into the same 3 objectives every time:

1. Remind the consumer to shop
2. Prompt the consumer to spend more than they bargained for
3. Force the consumer to buy something

With marketing able to profile down to the individual level of the consumer, one is bound to fall off, or be pulled off, of the no-shopping wagon and buy something on impulse. And that's OK. Mistakes are going to happen, it's one of the features that separate someone from being labeled a human being instead of a robot or computer. As I mentioned earlier, the key element to shifting a mistake from something bad to something good is to use the mistake as a learning tool. Understand what marketing strategy was successful in motivating you to shop, so you keep a look out for the same thing as it pops up in the future. In doing so, you can halt or redirect future attempts to prompt you to spend.

Marketing strategies place pressure on the consumer to buy in 2 ways, externally and internally. The tips and action steps in this chapter highlight the marketing strategies that I've fallen for in the past, as well as what I've done to stop them from affecting me in the future. It is my hope that these techniques will work for you too. I'll begin with the external forces.

Hit The Brakes:
Take defensive action on the outside forces that want you to shop

In the context of shopping addiction triggers, the external forces are the factors from the outside world that spark a person to shop. While marketers are largely responsible for the outside forces a consumer has to contend with, friends, family, and even co-workers can also contribute to igniting a desire to shop. The following 6 defensive actions have been designed to help you stay on course when external forces try to nudge you to impulse shop.

Defensive action #1—
Unsubscribe from catalogs and email savings offers

How many times an advertising message must remind a consumer to shop before they do so is called "effective frequency" and it's one of the holy grails of advertising. The more you touch the consumer the greater the chances are that they are going to purchase your product. If I receive a savings offer every single day then shopping is never going to leave my mind. Every savings offer, online advertisement, and coupon provided to me is a reminder for me to shop. Touch me enough times, and sooner or later, I'm going to crack. The only way to avoid this is to remove the reminders themselves. On my way out of a store I throw away coupons and survey offers for future savings. I unsubscribe from catalogs and emailed savings offers the moment they hit my inbox or mailbox. The less reminders that I have to shop, the less often that I will think about wanting something new, and the less the chance that I'll go shopping.

Defensive action #2—
Cancel rewards cards and savings programs

Rewards programs are built around a favorite strategy of marketers that I call "spend money to save money." A reward member receives credit for every dollar spent and these credits build up over time to trigger a savings offer. The customer information for rewards offers is stored electronically today, but in the past a check mark or hole punch was captured on a physical card that the customer kept in their wallet. One store I shopped in had a reward card where I received one hole punch for every $100 that I spent. When I had accumulated $100 in purchases 10 times, my next purchase of $100 was free. Saving $100, now that sounds like a nice savings! Except, I had to spent $100 ten times! That's $1,000! If I have to spend $1,000 to save $100, that's a mere 10% I'm saving. Suddenly the free $100 doesn't sound like it is that big of a savings anymore.

Defensive action #3—
Say no to freely giving out your personal information

If I don't give the store my personal information, then they can't contact me via email, postal mail, phone call, or text message, in other words they can't send me anything—ever. And if I don't have any reminders to shop, I'm going to think of doing it less often. Receiving a savings offer doesn't necessarily mean that I'm really going to save money if I use it. A savings offer only works if I was already intending to spend the money anyway. For example, if I signed up for a rewards card to save 20% on my purchase for that day, and my purchase total was $100, I would have saved $20. Not a bad number to save. But if I receive an offer to save another 20% a week later, I may think about what I can purchase to save another 20%. And if I didn't need another $100 worth of merchandise, than the $20 I "saved" from making a second purchase was really money that I didn't save at all because I wasn't going to shop again so soon.

The first 3 defensive actions have the same intention in mind—remove the ability for a retailer to remind you to shop. But it's not the only strategy that retailers use on customers.

Defensive action #4—
Spend what you want to spend

Another commonly used marketing strategy is to prompt the consumer to spend more than they bargained for. I call this "spending to save." Unlike the earlier strategy "spend money to save money," in this situation there is no rewards program to join and I don't have to wait to become eligible for the savings offer. This time I can save money the very same day I'm buying something, if, and only if, I spend a certain amount at the time of purchase. Two common "spending to save" offers are to "spend $100 and save $50" and to get free shipping on my order after I've spent a specific dollar amount. At first glance these offers look like a really good deal, I'm already going to spend my money, so why not get a little something extra for it, right? For example, if I spend $100 I'll get an item for half off because I can save 50% off of my total. This appears like a good deal, but sometimes appearances can be deceiving.

Often I would easily find 1 item in the store that I wanted, and its price would always be lower than $100. For example, I find something with a price of $39.50. OK great, only $60.50 more to spend and I'll save my $50. But then I would run right into a hurdle, I would struggle to find a second item that was exactly $60.50. Items would be $39.50, or $49.50, or $59.50, but nothing would be $60.50. Well what am I supposed to do now? Easy, I'll just purchase 3 items for $39.50 each.

$39.50 per item X 3 items = $118.50 total purchase

But the savings offer was "spend $100 and save $50," which means that I'm only going to save $50 off of a purchase of $100. My total purchase was $118.50, which means that I am $18.50 over the $100 limit. I'll end up spending a total of $68.50 instead of the $50 I thought I would spend when I heard about the savings offer. This is because I couldn't find 2 items that equaled exactly $100, I had to go over $100 to get the savings offer.

$118.50 total purchase – $50 savings offer = $68.50 new total purchase

My final purchase not only put me over budget, I spent $68.50 instead of $50, but also, I walked away with 3 new items. More often than not, I only intended to walk away with 1 or 2, not 3 or more.

Sometimes the "spending to save" offer is based on item number instead of total purchase price, especially when looking at socks and undergarments. Common rewards offers are "purchase 3, get 1 free" or "purchase 3 for $33 or $14.50 each."

Once again the offer initially sounds like a great deal. If I were to purchase 3 items without the savings offer I would spend:

Full price purchase = $14.50 each X 3 items = $43.50 total purchase

Comparing to the savings offer, for the same 3 items I will now spend:

Savings offer purchase = 3 for $33.00 is $33.00 ÷ 3 or $11.00 each

With the savings offer, I am able to save $10.50, that's almost 1 pair for free. By purchasing 3 items to get the savings, I would spend less money than if I purchased the 3 items at full price. So where's the problem? Well, what if I only needed 2 items? Now I am once again going over, this time for both number of items *and* total money spent. If I had stuck to my original plan, to purchase 2 items, I could have spent less money *and* walked out of the store with only the items I really needed.

Full price purchase = $14.50 x 2 items = $29.00 total purchase = 2 items

versus

Savings offer purchase = 3 for $33.00 = 3 items

I may have spent more per item by purchasing less, but if my budget only allowed for 2 items, at $29.00, I did not have to overspend by $4.00 and walk out of the store with an extra item I did not intend to purchase.

The allure of saving money is very attractive to most shoppers, easily turning into a game—how many things can I buy and how much can I save while doing it—which is why this strategy is often used. It's also the reason why it's so important to make sure you decide up front what you want to buy, and how much you want to spend, *before* you walk into a store. The Shopping Plan Worksheet in Chapter 6 was designed to help you when making these decisions so that you'll stay focused on buying the stuff that you *need*, and not stuff that you *want* simply because the savings offer looked tempting.

Defensive action #5—
Ask for gift cards for retailers who sell disposable goods or that can be used anywhere

One industry that has grown considerably in the past 20 years is gift cards. Holidays, birthdays, weddings, giveaways, regardless of the occasion, gift cards have become a standard option. Yet despite their rising popularity and convenience, gift cards carry with them many downfalls—expiration dates, fees, and most important of all—obligation. In order to use the gift card, you have to go to the retailer to use it. Now, there have been times when I've received a gift card for a store that I was already planning to visit, and the gift card amount covers the total purchase price of what I planned to buy. In those cases receiving a gift card was a welcome obligation, because I was going to buy anyway.

However, getting gift cards at the right time doesn't always happen. I've also received quite a few gift cards where the obligation to shop became a burden, because I felt forced to buy. I'll get a gift card for a store that I thought I liked and then "wham!" For some mysterious reason I go to the store and I can no longer find *anything* in the store that I want. I walk out empty handed and frustrated, while the gift card sits in my wallet, day after day, and eventually week after week, unused. With a strong desire to spend, I will continuously surf the retailer's website, or visit the store in person, searching for something, anything, to purchase, so that I can use my gift card. And sooner or later, I will feel pressured to just get rid of the darn gift card already and I'll buy something that I don't want, motivated by the simple fact that I no longer want to hold the gift card in my wallet.

Gift cards also set up a shopper for the "spend to save" trap mentioned earlier in this chapter. I walk into a store with a gift card, pick the things I want to buy, and find myself with leftover money on the gift card. What do I do now? Why I spend it all, of course. With this goal in mind, I'll select random items, just enough stuff to cover the rest of the gift card. Unfortunately, in my haste to spend it all, I typically end up walking out of a store with things I didn't really want to buy, and most times I'll even have to shell out some of my own cash to cover the total purchase price too. I bought more than I wanted and spent more than I planned, all so I could redeem the gift card.

The only way to prevent an obligation to shop at a retailer is to decline gift cards. Declining a gift card is one option, but it's not something that's going to work for me. I like receiving gift cards. What I do instead is avoid asking for gift cards to clothing stores, since those stores are a trigger for me. Instead, my gift card requests are for the retailers that carry disposable items that I use all the time: grocery stores, coffee shops, gas stations, etc as well as large retailers, such as Amazon, Walmart, and Target, that stock a variety of products and consumable goods including books and music. Another option is to request a gift card that can be used universally, such as a VISA or American Express gift card. Finally, gift cards to retailers come with the added benefit that you can store the gift card as credit on the website with no expiration date, enabling you to spend when you are ready to.

Defensive action #6—
Focus on the need, not the brand

Two terms that are often used interchangeably in the marketing, advertising, and business industries, but have distinct differences are brand and branding. The American Marketing Association defines a brand as the "name, term, design, symbol, or any other feature that identifies one seller's good or service as distinct from those of other sellers."[11] In other words, the brand tells you the source

[11] American Marketing Association Dictionary. Brand. Available at: https://www.ama.org/resources/Pages/Dictionary.aspx?dLetter=B&dLetter=B. Accessed: November 17, 2016.

of the product. Branding is the art of aligning the source of the product with a lasting impression in the customer's mind. The goal of many marketing strategies is to carve out a specific set of qualities and attributes that you'll think about when you see or hear about a brand. For example, if I were to ask you to tell me 2 attributes about FedEx, what would you say? Speed and efficiency. What about Target? Affordable chic. How about Starbucks? Personalized service. Your answers may differ from mine, but I'm willing to bet that for at least one of these companies you were able to provide a short, descriptive answer. Your answers were formed on the basis of your interpretation about the company, that is, your personal opinion about the brand.

Back in Chapter 1, I mentioned that one of the key elements of shopping is emotional motivation. Too often I've let my emotional response to owning something by a specific brand, and not my needs, drive my decision to buy. And every time I have made a decision based on brand alone, I've ended up adding stuff to my wardrobe that doesn't work out well for me.

For example, the Frye boot company claims to be the longest continuously operating shoe company in the United States. Frye prides itself on history, heritage, and craftsmanship. As a lover of boots, I have always wanted to own a pair of Frye's. When I stumbled across a pair of tall, taupe Frye boots, in my size at an end-of-season sale price, I had to own them. After all, they were Frye's, they were in my size, and they were on sale! I trapsed through the mall with my shopping bag, which was too small for the box holding my new boots, but I didn't care. I finally owned my very own pair of Frye boots. When I stopped for a cup of tea, a stranger noticed my Frye boot box peeking out of my shopping bag and asked about them. I was more than happy to pull them out of the box and show off my new Frye's. I had not owned them for more than an hour and here I was, already getting praise from strangers on my new boots. Surely they were meant to be.

When the fall season rolled around and I was finally able to start wearing my new Frye's I ran into a few complications. The boots were an awkward length, the height hitting me right in the knee cap. Attempting to work with the length, I rolled the top down to create a cuff. I didn't care for the cuffed look, but I was wearing Frye's so who cares, right? Another snag I ran into was the color itself. The boots were taupe, a color that didn't coordinate well with my wardrobe. Every time I tried to assemble an outfit with my new Frye's I'd end up having to settle for something else because the boots just didn't work. I bought the Frye boots because of the label, but I never considered the fit, the color, or how well they would, or in this case would not, coordinate with my existing wardrobe. I ended up donating those boots after wearing them a mere 3 or 4 times. To this day, I still want to own a pair of Frye boots, but I've learned my lesson. If I ever purchase a pair again, they have to be a size, color, and style that will work well with my wardrobe, instead of fighting against it. I have many shopping stories like this.

In this situation it was the label and not the features of the item itself that was the reason for my purchase. Too often I've bought pieces because I wanted to own an item by a specific designer. And more often than not, the purchase hasn't worked well for me, because I didn't buy the item with a focus on how well the piece fit my current body, lifestyle, and wardrobe. Now when I shop I ignore the label and let my needs—not the brand—determine what I buy.

Thus far I've discussed 6 defensive measures against the external forces trying to tempt you to buy when you don't really want to. Now I'm going to move on to steps that you can do to halt the pressure that comes from the inside.

Hit The Brakes:
Keep an eye on your internal dialogue

In the context of a shopping addiction, the internal dialogue is the thinking process inside a person's head that sparks them to shop. Sometimes this inner voice has developed as a direct result of marketing messages. Other times the inner voice is nothing more than a gut feeling. Regardless of the source, the following 5 internal actions have been designed to help you navigate around inner thoughts trying to encourage you to shop.

Internal action #1—
Own only one to keep it special

Back in the 1990s, Coach had established itself as a luxury leather goods and accessories brand. The average, middle-income household knew what the Coach brand was, but many of these customers didn't own a Coach bag. Then in the early 2000s, leather alternatives and logo patterns became popular and the lower cost of goods allowed Coach to develop a marketing strategy centered around a nylon bag with a C pattern, at an affordable price point. This one product became a big hit and Coach handbags took off like a rocket, leading to the expansion from 50 retail stores in the US, to more than 1,000 stores across multiple continents, as well as the addition of outlet stores. Coach had recreated themselves from a "luxury brand" available only to a select few, to an "affordable luxury brand" available to middle-income households.

I remember when I received my first Coach bag, it was a small, black, all-leather handbag, with a zipper closure. I was thrilled! I finally had a luxury handbag of my own. I sported that handbag every single day, and I felt like a million bucks. But then something happened, I received a second Coach handbag. This time in brown leather, with a snap closure. Well, if I felt like a million bucks with the first one, then owning 2 bags meant that I should feel like 2 million bucks, right? Wrong. Instead of becoming happy that I owned 2, I was torn. I started swapping my handbags, coordinating my bags with my outfits.

Then something absurd happened, I received a third handbag. Then I purchased a fourth one myself. Before I knew it, I owned half a dozen Coach handbags. With this development something else happened, the bags no longer felt special. Owning a Coach handbag became my new normal. My handbag collection had morphed from one filled with $20 and $30 bags to $200 and $300 bags.

With Coach handbags no longer special, I began to crave a new special handbag brand. But the craving for something new and special brought with it a downside—a higher price point. If $200 and $300 handbags were no longer going to be special then I was going to need a more expensive bag. My tastes shifted to a new luxury brand, Louis Vuitton. And this change in palate brought with it a higher price tag. My new, special, Louis Vuitton bag did not cost a mere $200 to $300, it cost over $1,000. And when I finally received my first Louis Vuitton handbag, what do you think happened? That's right, I wanted another one.

When you stop keeping a handbag (or any other wardrobe item) special, 2 things can happen. First, you may start to crave something new, which will increase the number of items in your wardrobe. Second, the price point of the desired item goes up, causing you to spend more money to feel special again. But if you own only 1, you may feel less inclined to shop for a replacement item, and more importantly—you'll keep the item special.

Internal action #2—
Shop for OUTFITS that you LOVE, not ITEMS that you LIKE

If I'm in a store, I see it, I like it, and it fits well, I'm going to want it. But liking something is not the only reason why I should decide to buy something. I like a *lot* of things! I'm always going to find something in a store that I like. A pair of shoes, a necklace, a handbag, a blouse, a shirt, a pair of jeans or boots, with all of the variety available today, it's easy to find things that I like.

Back in Chapter 5 I discussed the 5 factors that make up your personal style—fashion style, dressing preference, signature color, body type, and lifestyle. Knowing and sticking to clothes that align with your personal style will have a considerable impact on your shopping habits and how well your wardrobe will (or will not) support your dressing needs.

To my eye, prints stand out faster than a solid and they are often the first thing I notice in a store. Except my personal style doesn't include a lot of prints, and the prints I do wear are usually fairly simple, dots or lines. If I walk around a store and only buy prints that catch my eye I'm going to be left with a lot of printed items that I can't create into an outfit. After all, I'm not the type of person to sport an outfit that's head-to-toe prints, I'll temper the print with a solid. For example, a striped shirt with a pair of denim blue jeans or a dotted blouse with a black trouser. Only buying prints that I like will quickly leave me with a closet filled with half outfits, printed tops and bottoms that I won't wear together. I'm going to need some solids to complete my look. But if I focus on shopping for outfits that I love, I'll focus on adding the necessary items to allow me to be able to sport my newly loved print, and I'll end up owning a closet filled with things that I love, and am able to use. That's why when you shop you have to make sure that you are buying outfits you will love to wear, instead of items that you'd like to own.

Internal action #3—
Track and acknowledge your progress, no matter how big or small

In the 5th century, a lengthy poem about heroic deeds and events called *Psychomachia* (or *Battle of spirits*), was written in the narrative style by the poet Aurelius Prudentius Clemens. The poem discusses the battle between virtues and vices. The proverbial phrase "patience is a virtue" refers back to one of the 7 heavenly virtues from *Psychomachia*. An individual with patience is said to have high moral standards, a character trait that is rarely found in most people. And for a very good reason: it is not easy to be patient! When trying to change overshopping behavior, displaying self-control becomes increasingly harder to do. The passage of time brings with it the potential for discouragement, and when this occurs, moving along the path to progress stops as suddenly as hitting a brick wall going 50 mph.

When walking along the road to change, it is often helpful to break up a large goal into smaller, more achievable stepping stones. In doing so, something that at first appears overwhelming and unmanageable is turned into that which can be attained. While participating in The DH Closet Challenge, mentioned back in Chapter 4, a portion of my wardrobe sat in the "boutique," essentially on hold, unworn, for many, many months, 18 months to be exact. Multiple times during that 18-month period, I found myself digging around in the boutique. I spent hours analyzing and criticizing the clothes that sat unworn. Time and again I would try to push myself to get rid of pieces. Clothes would move into the donate bag, and then back out again, over and over. In the bag, out of the bag, in the bag, out of the bag, it was like watching a tennis match. Every time I would add something to the donate bag, I would pull it back out, because I just wasn't ready to let go of the clothes that were on hold. As the months passed, the boutique developed into a dead weight hanging over my head.

During The DH Closet Challenge I grew to despise the boutique. Every time I looked at the items stored in there, I saw evidence of wasted money and an out-of-control shopping habit. I was embarrassed that I owned a large number of clothes that I was not using regularly. I was also frustrated that I could not get rid of everything in one fell swoop. I had completely forgotten the point of The DH Closet Challenge— to help me reduce the size of my wardrobe, so that I would be happy with my clothes. Instead I became miserable, obsessed with the boutique and all of the clothes that I was not using.

To prevent myself from continuing to spiral out of control I turned to photos. When I began The DH Closet Challenge and created the boutique, I took photos of how much clothing sat inside. Periodically during the course of the challenge, I would manage to donate a bag of clothes from the boutique. I photographed those bags, and once again photographed the new, smaller boutique. Having before and after pictures allowed me to visually track my progress over time. In the beginning, there wasn't much of a difference between the before and after photos. But over time, I made enough progress to notice it, and that's when my mood changed from frustration with what I still owned, to joy that the boutique was growing smaller over time.

In addition to taking photos, I looked closely for other signs of progress, no matter how small they were. When I purged a small handful of items, I acknowledged that clothes were no longer piled up double (or triple) on a hanger. As garments left the boutique I began to notice the space between the clothing on the closet rod increased in size. It became easier to reach in and pull something out, without 3 others getting dragged along with it.

I also started to pay attention to the condition of the clothes that went into the donation bag. In the beginning, the majority of my purged clothing was in new condition, complete with the store tags still on it. As time passed, less and less clothing had store tags on them. In its place sat garments that were still in fair condition, but had clearly been worn more than once. About 7 to 8 months into The DH Closet Challenge something monumental occurred: I removed a shirt from my wardrobe but instead of adding it to the donate bag, I had to place it in the trash bin, the shirt had holes in it! I also had to discard a pair of shoes because the soles fell apart. During the course of The DH Closet Challenge, I began to wear out my clothing, instead of getting rid of items merely because I owned too many.

When progress is moving at the pace of a snail, it is difficult to acknowledge that any gains are made. Sometimes the changes are small, almost unnoticeable. To help keep you motivated to push through the times when it looks like nothing is changing, focus on the little milestones that happen. Staying consistent with tracking results and shopping habits will help keep you from falling off the wagon and becoming discouraged.

Internal action #4—
Remind yourself of your goals

Going hand in hand with tracking progress is making sure that you remind yourself what the end goal is. Incorporating daily reminders of your end goal will help motivate you to keep pushing when change feels like it's moving too slow, or the task at hand appears really difficult to do.

What a person uses for motivation will be different from one individual to the next. For myself I choose 3 different ways to remind myself about my end goal:

1. DH's personal closet
2. A postcard from France
3. Minimalism websites, blogs, and forums

1. **DH's personal closet.** DH's closet was a great source of motivation because the closet was similar to the one I wanted for myself. DH's wardrobe accurately portrays his lifestyle; the bulk of his clothing is dedicated to work, which is where he spends 5 of his 7 days per week. And he regularly wears every single one of these pieces. He has the appropriate outfit for occasions as they arise throughout the year. There is plenty of space between hangers on the closet rod and among the items on the shelves. The only garments in a holding zone are sentimental and they can be counted on one hand. He sports items until they are worn out and only purchases what he needs regardless of the offers in the store. I will often peek inside DH's personal closet to remind myself of the type of wardrobe I want for myself—small, versatile, and well-utilized.

2. **A postcard from France.** A close friend gave me a postcard from France that I kept taped to a mirror that I used every day while dressing. This postcard reminded me of French wardrobes and shopping philosophies, which is something I sought to keep

in mind for myself. I adored the stereotypical idea that a French closet is filled with few items compared with the standard American closet. The French wardrobe consists of high-quality classic pieces that are worn regularly. Articles discussing French wardrobes often portray the French shopper as someone who only purchases those garments that they had pre-planned to purchase, and the new additions always complement the shopper's wardrobe and current lifestyle. During my visits abroad I've witnessed women carrying high-end designer handbags or sporting shoes and boots that no longer looked like they had come fresh off the retail shelf. Materials were broken in, leather had darkened over time, and the soles of shoes were marked from use. I was confused. If someone spent a lot of money on an item, wouldn't they want to keep it looking "like new"? Why would you want a $1,000 handbag to get dirty, or wear out the red sole on an $800 shoe? Simple, because these women loved what they owned, and what better way to showcase that you love something, than to actually *use it*.

I rarely see these same features among designer bags and footwear among women in the US. Everything always looks shiny and new. The postcard from France acted as a reminder of the philosophies and behavior from the French wardrobe style that I admire and to continue to seek out this behavior for myself—own less and use it more often.

3. **Minimalism websites, blogs, and forums.** Reviewing and participating in websites, blogs, and forums with a nod towards minimalism helps keep me on my toes. Unlike the prior 2 sources of motivation, internet-based sources are updated often, sometimes even daily. This not only keeps the idea of streamlining my wardrobe top of mind but also keeps me thinking about new ways that I may be able to keep moving forward with my goals. Learning about a community that is dedicated to owning and doing more with less has been a great source of motivation. It is helpful to know that I'm not alone in my desire for wanting less or with encountering obstacles while moving towards my goals.

Internal action #5—
Make the time and commitment to change

What is one thing that all top athletes have in common regardless of which sport they do? Practice. Training sessions provide value in a number of ways: existing skill sets are fine-tuned, teammate camaraderie is strengthened, and the repetitive nature of training sessions leads to new formations and game plans becoming second nature. Changing a shopping habit is no different. Before I could permanently alter my shopping ways, I had to make the time to do so. I had to practice shopping in a new way. On one particular day I might set aside 5 minutes to change my behavior and my only goal was to use the computer and *not* visit a retailers' website during that 5-minute period. Other days I would dedicate a couple of hours to visit a mall, my goal to spend time inside retail stores without buying anything. On other occasions I devoted 30 minutes inside my closet, reviewing my wardrobe to see if I am ready, willing, and able to move items into the donation bag. Regardless of the length of time, I made sure to set aside designated periods where I focused on changing my behavior. I couldn't grow and learn from my mistakes if I never gave myself an opportunity to do so, which meant I had to set aside dedicated time to practice changing my shopping habits. Athletes practice for their chosen sport, and I practice to become better at shopping and managing my personal wardrobe.

What drives an athlete to practice day after day, repeating the same motions again and again until their skills become fine-tuned? Commitment. As I studied myself moving through the 4 elements of shopping back in Chapter 1, I realized that I had an addiction to shopping. At that time, I made the decision that I wanted to stop overshopping. I wanted to stop owning a wardrobe that I hated. I wanted to stop buying stuff that didn't work for me. I wanted to change. And as I've stated in the beginning of this chapter, the pathway to change is often a long, winding road, filled with highs and lows. Setbacks can and do occur. The only thing that will get someone past a roadblock is staying committed to working towards the end goal, no matter how long it takes or how many obstacles pop up.

Just how long and how many obstacles can pop up while trying to change? In the case of myself, it took me 4 years to shop an annual sale successfully! Here's what happened.

Case study—Shopping an annual sale

My favorite retailer conducts a sale that has become legendary among its customers, and this particular sale only happens once per year, in the middle of July. The sale consists of the fall merchandise that is brand new for the upcoming season, at prices reduced 10% to 55% off, for only 2 weeks. Once the sale period is over, the prices return to full retail until the end of the season. The fact that the merchandise available for purchase consists of the latest designs, colors, and styles, and not leftovers from a prior season, is what makes this particular sale unique compared with the usual sales offered by retailers.

I've watched award shows and seen the celebrities sporting styles straight off the runway. These lucky ladies and men are wearing looks on the red carpet before the clothes are available in retail stores. Now, thanks to this sale, for 2 weeks I am offered the chance to become a part of this select group of people, wearing the newest fall styles at the start of the season, and at a discount!

The potential to own something for the upcoming fall season before anyone else, coupled with the incentive to acquire designer items at rare discounted pricing, makes this sale my favorite sale throughout the year. Unfortunately, these features also meant that, with my overshopper tendencies, this sale was the most challenging sale for me to attend. In fact, it took me 4 years to learn how to shop the sale successfully. Why did it take me such a long time to shop a simple sale? Easy; I made a lot of mistakes before I figured out what to do right.

Year One

The first year I didn't realize I had an addiction to shopping and it showed in my behavior at the yearly sale. I shopped like a starving lioness let loose into the wild with food running all around. Knee-high gray boots, score! Multi-print blouse, mine! Designer denim jeans, absolutely! I made a lot of random purchases, selecting whatever caught my eye. The only thought in my mind was that these items were the latest and greatest "must have's" for the season. I was thrilled to be on the forefront of fashion with my new items. After all, this was new merchandise, already on sale! In a few short weeks, everything would be back to full price and I'd already own these items at a discount.

My shopping strategy of "I like it, it's on sale, I'm buying it" didn't work out very well. The tall gray boots were hard to coordinate with my tops and bottoms.

The multi-print blouse was lovely, but as a knit gal, it sat unworn in favor of other pieces. The designer denim jeans were great, but I wasn't wearing all 3 new pairs! I always reached for the same pair. Overall the bulk of my must have finds from my first yearly sale sat unworn the entire season, until I eventually purged the stuff out of my wardrobe.

Year Two

By the time the second year rolled around I had finally accepted that fact that I struggled with an addiction to shopping. To help me manage my shopping habits I decided that I would shop this yearly sale with a strategy. I would shop for *all* of my fall/winter needs during the sale. Why? One of the hallmarks of an overshopper is shopping often. I figured if I only shopped for the fall/winter season during the sale, I would have reigned in my shopping beast because I'd only shop 1 time, for both fall and winter. This didn't work very well for me, because I'm a graze shopper, not a gorge shopper! I also didn't write a shopping list ahead of time, which was a really big mistake. Instead of enjoying the sale, I agonized over every single item. Will I really need that new blazer? I don't know, but if I don't purchase it now, I'll be stuck all season without a new blazer. Is that scarf really necessary? I don't know about the rest of my wardrobe, but it matches that new blazer, so I better pick it up. I have to purchase that dress on sale, *now*. It's the only dress in the sale that flatters me, and I won't be able to buy any more once the sale is over, so better to be safe than sorry.

I struggled to buy stuff that would work well for my wardrobe and I ended up walking away having spent and added more than I had the previous year. Yikes! The massive amount of stuff that I bought left me with yet another fragmented wardrobe for the season.

Year Three

By the third year I had been making great strides in managing my shopping addiction and approached the sale with a new plan. I really wanted to make sure that I shopped with a list so that I didn't haphazardly grab everything on the racks in my size. I decided to use the sale as a way to freshen up my fall/winter wardrobe. The first day of the sale, I perused the items. Then I went home and crafted a list based on what I had seen. My goal was to purchase only the items on my list. I sport lots of blazers, and the newest style, bomber jackets looked like a nice alternative, so I added that to my list. I wear blue denim jeans daily, and the colored and printed options seemed like a nice way to jazz up my denim, so those were included. I didn't already own a black leather jacket, and I found a flattering option on sale, so I added that to the list too.

I walked away from year 3 having stuck to my list and buying only those items that I intended to buy. Compared with years 1 and 2, I had made great progress. I bought and returned fewer items overall, and I really enjoyed the things that I bought. Yet my wardrobe was still not functioning properly after the sale. I once again struggled to create outfit combinations that I enjoyed. How was this possible? Pretty easy actually. I had filled my closet with items that I liked and would "freshen up" my wardrobe. And that was the problem. My only plan was to "freshen up" my wardrobe. Everything that I added was outside of my usual style and comfort zone; I had forgotten about my personal style!

Year Four

By year 4 my addiction to shopping was under control and I *finally* figured out how to shop the yearly sale. I added items to my wardrobe that became workhorse pieces throughout the fall season. And it was easy for me to assemble outfits with my new wardrobe additions. It had taken me 4 years, but my persistence to keep changing how I shopped and keep trying eventually led me to shop the sale successfully. I also walked away from my fourth year having developed a 3-step approach that I still use today to shop this yearly sale. These steps are a condensed form of the shopping plan discussed in Chapter 6:

1. Look in my closet
2. Write my shopping list
3. Do the research

Here's a closer look at each of the 3 steps.

1. **Look in my closet.** Unlike the prior years, when I began with the sale as my starting point for what to add in my wardrobe, for year 4, I started with what was inside my current fall/winter wardrobe instead. I reviewed what I already had to figure out what was still missing. I carefully analyzed every individual garment that was left in my closet from the last fall/winter season. Anything that no longer fit my current size, was worn out, torn, stained or otherwise damaged, or I just didn't want to wear for another season was removed. This process resulted in the removal of 16 garments from my closet. With 16 items removed from my wardrobe, and deciding to adhere to the one in/one out rule, gave me the opportunity to shop the sale for a total of 16 new items. But, should I really purchase 16 new things? To help me answer this question I moved on to step 2.

2. **Write my shopping list.** To create my list of wardrobe holes/needs, I took a long hard look at what I had removed from my closet, and identified the function of each item. Then I searched the remainder of my wardrobe, to see if I already had a suitable replacement. For example, if I donated my horseback riding shirts, did I still own a shirt to use for horseback riding or did I need to shop for a new one, since I had nothing left? After noting

the clothes and shoes I wanted based on function, I assessed what was missing from my closet to help me complete an outfit. Once again, I reviewed what was left in my fall closet, except this time, my review required me to take each garment, and assemble it into an outfit. Every time I ran into a stumbling block to complete a look, I jotted down what I would need to finish the outfit. Closely reviewing my existing closet and identifying what the wardrobe holes/needs were helped arm myself with a targeted list to use when I shopped. Once I finished writing my list, I discovered that I didn't need 16 replacement items for my fall/winter wardrobe. Curious how many items were on my shopping list that year? Nine, that's right, only 9.

3. **Do the research.** Now that I knew what I was looking for, I shopped the sale searching for the pieces on my shopping list. I only found 8 of my 9 shopping list items at the sale. For the wardrobe item the sale didn't have, I waited until the next wave of merchandise arrived in the stores a few months later. By reviewing what I already had, and determining ahead of time what I was looking for, I was able to stop shopping the sale solely for items that "caught my eye." Instead I had an action plan to ensure that my shopping sessions were productive and resulted in wardrobe additions that enhanced my wardrobe, instead of burdening it. Because I did

all of my research on the internet, and sometimes pieces on my computer screen look vastly different in person, I had given myself a "wildcard item" on my shopping list, something I could buy that I didn't pre-plan. I actually walked away from this sale with 2 wildcard items, for a total of 10 new pieces overall for my fall/winter wardrobe.

Learning the proper way to shop was a long and difficult process. I didn't change my habits overnight, it took years of hard work, and many wins and failures along the way. And while wins are always preferred, it is actually the failures that provide the information necessary to craft an action plan to achieve the desired change.

When setbacks occur, they don't signal the end of the journey. Forgive yourself for your mistakes, recommit to making a change, create a plan, and then proceed to move forward. Eventually the change will come, and because you're consciously aware of the fact that you are trying to make a change, when it does happen, you'll be able to recognize it, and pat yourself on the back for a job well done. Then once you've achieved your goal—owning a wardrobe that you love—it's time to have a little fun with what's inside.

Chapter 9 recap:

Mistakes are just opportunities to make a change.

 Hit The Brakes:
Take defensive action on the outside forces that want you to shop

- Remove the ability for a retailer to remind you to shop by:
  1. Unsubscribing from catalogs and email savings offers
  2. Canceling rewards cards and savings programs
  3. Saying "no" to freely giving out your personal information
- Avoid having to spend more than you planned by:
  1. Deciding in advance how much you want to spend
  2. Asking for gift cards to retailers who sell disposable goods or that can be used anywhere
  3. Focusing on the need the item will fulfill, not the brand itself

 Hit The Brakes:
Keep an eye on your internal dialogue

- Stop your thoughts from triggering you to spend by:
  1. Keeping an item special by owning only 1
  2. Shopping for outfits that you love, not items that you like

3. Tracking and acknowledging your progress, no matter how big or small it may be
4. Often reminding yourself of your goals, by using pictures, the example of others, websites, blogs, forums, etc
5. Making the time and commitment to change, especially when roadblocks pop up that try to throw you off course

The only way that failure is truly an option is if you give up. When a relapse occurs, use it as a sign of what you need to change, then develop a plan so that you are prepared for the next time the trigger rolls around again.

Chapter 10

Inventive ways to get your money's worth out of your clothes

Enjoying what you have is one of the secrets to happiness

Every chapter in this book has been focused on helping you assemble a wardrobe filled with items that you love and can use in your daily life—until now. Coming up with different outfit options and using more of your wardrobe is the focus of this final chapter. Shaping your wardrobe to hold pieces that you love is a lot of hard work, and now that you've laid the foundation for your wardrobe, it's time to have a little fun with the stuff that you own. When all of your attention is centered on understanding, streamlining, and using more of your wardrobe, it's sometimes easy to forget about what the end goal of all of this hard work is supposed to be—to enjoy what's inside your closet!

Sometimes a person can own a wardrobe that meets all of their needs, yet they still carry a nagging feeling that something about their wardrobe just isn't right. The wardrobe doesn't feel "finished" despite the physical evidence to the contrary. This is exactly what happened to me. I had stopped shopping mindlessly and finally shaped my wardrobe into the perfect wardrobe for me, and I was still unhappy about it. How was this possible? Isn't the end result of this journey to love my wardrobe? If I love everything that I own, why aren't I happy about it? I was so close to the end goal, but I had once again gotten stuck. I didn't know how to find happiness with my new found success.

If you are like me, when you've spent years unhappy with your wardrobe, in order to achieve happiness about what you own, you have to overcome the cycle of wardrobe dissatisfaction (Figure 9).

Figure 9: *The Cycle of Wardrobe Dissatisfaction*

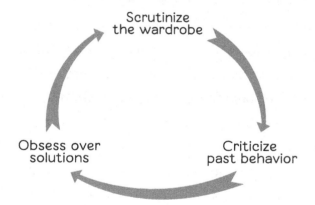

The cycle of wardrobe dissatisfaction occurs when someone has gotten used to living in a state of unhappiness about their wardrobe. I had gotten stuck in a rut because I was used to focusing on my negative behavior. I'd been working on fixing my wardrobe and my shopping habits for so long, I didn't realize that the day would come when I didn't have to anymore.

To achieve long-term happiness with my wardrobe, my attention had to shift towards what my closet *could* do, instead of remaining fixated on what my closet was *not* doing. Now that I owned a wardrobe filled with the right clothes for my lifestyle, my personal style, and my body size, the time had come to participate in a new cycle for my behavior, one whose goal was reinforcing joy and contentment, not frustration and dissatisfaction, with what was inside my wardrobe. I had to shift my thoughts away from the critique of the negatives and into acknowledging the positives about my clothes. I had to learn to be happy with what I owned—to start *enjoying* what I owned. If any of this sounds familiar, well then the solution for me just might work well for you too. The way that I learned to start enjoying my clothes was to participate in a wardrobe challenge.

Hit The Brakes:
Participate in a wardrobe challenge
to have fun with your wardrobe

Wardrobe challenges let you experience how much fun you can have with your wardrobe by allowing you to see what your wardrobe can do, instead of focusing on analyzing what your wardrobe lacks. Focusing on the good about my wardrobe, instead of the bad within it, kept me satisfied with what I owned instead of wanting to continue searching for and buying new pieces to make me happy. With the wardrobe challenges in this chapter you can test your wardrobe's size, flexibility, and creativity. And when you find yourself stuck, or you are simply unable to select a challenge to do, well I have a challenge for that situation too. So grab your calendar, a notepad, and a pen, and let's have a little fun with your wardrobe.

Wardrobe challenge #1—
Limit items and days

If you were to run a search on the internet for wardrobe challenges, the most popular challenge you'd find is an item challenge. 30 items for 30 days, 33 items for 3 months, 60 items for 60 days, 1 item for 1 year, etc. The number of items and the time frame may vary, but the rules of an item challenge are pretty straightforward. You select a predetermined number of clothes (and sometimes shoes and accessories too) and use only that number for a prespecified length of time. That's all there is to it. If you are someone looking for a challenge that requires an initial set-up period, followed by a moderate length challenge period, or you are simply interested in testing out a minimalist wardrobe, then this is the challenge for you. Here's what happened when I participated in an item challenge.

Case study—30 items for 30 days

The plan: As the challenge says, pick 30 wardrobe items and use only those items for 30 days.

The wardrobe: To assemble this challenge wardrobe I split the total number of items allowed into 2 equal parts: 15 tops/toppers and 15 bottoms for 30 days. I began by selecting my favorite cardigans, blazers, jackets, and sweaters, added 1 top for each day of the week, and finished off the capsule with the bulk of the bottoms in my wardrobe. At the time of this challenge, I still had skirts and dresses in my wardrobe, therefore I made sure to include them as well. Dresses are unique wardrobe items because they function as both a top and a bottom, all from 1 garment, therefore, a dress works double-duty and can be placed in both the tops and bottoms categories.

I didn't include outerwear, undergarments, or shoes in my challenge wardrobe totals. I kept mostly solid pieces for my challenge wardrobe, however, I did include a few prints to add some interest to outfits without the need for accessories. My challenge wardrobe is listed in Table 10.

Table 10: *My Wardrobe for the 30 Items for 30 Days Challenge*

Toppers (8)	Tops (7)	Bottoms (15)
Navy Blazer	Plaid Shirt	Blue Bootcut Jeans
Black Cardigan	White Shirt	Blue Skinny Jeans
Ivory Sweater	Ivory Long-sleeve T-shirt	Black Skinny Jeans
Denim Jacket	White T-shirt	Black Bootcut Jeans
Army Green Jacket	Black Knit	White Skinny Jeans
Ivory Printed Cardigan	Black Sheath Dress	Black Sheath Dress
Black Blazer	Denim Shirt	White Bootcut Jeans
Black Cable Turtleneck		Black Trousers
		Black Pencil Skirt
		Denim Skirt
		Cobalt Straight Leg Jeans
		Green Skinny Jeans
		Light Blue Bootcut Jeans
		Blue Bootcut Jeans
		Brown Skinny Jeans

I walked away from this challenge with 7 key insights about my personal preferences:

1. **Dresses are highly versatile.** Dresses have the reputation of being an extremely versatile wardrobe item. And indeed, they are. When I started planning my outfits, I realized that a dress serves a dual role in an outfit, it's both the top and the bottom which provides a few outfit options. A dress can be worn on its own, layered with a top so that only the bottom half is shown, giving the illusion of a skirt, or layered underneath a longer skirt so that only the top half is shown, giving the illusion of a top.

2. **Skirts and dresses are not for everyone.** I discovered that I was not a fan of skirts or dresses. I didn't sport either option even one time throughout the 30-day challenge period. I used this observation to purge or donate all of the skirts and dresses from my everyday wardrobe at the end of the challenge period.

3. **Not everything mixes easily within a wardrobe.** A small handful of items didn't remix easily with the pieces in my challenge wardrobe. I called these items "1 outfit wonders." These outlier items were taking up valuable space in my wardrobe, yet their usefulness was very low. I think it's OK to own a handful of pieces that don't remix with most of the items in one's wardrobe, but when I own a lot of these stand-alone pieces, I'm left

with a low percentage of clothing items that can remix into new outfit combinations. And if I crave a lot of variety for my outfits, I may become tempted to shop because I can't create a new outfit combination with what I already own, which leaves me wanting something new to fulfill my need for variety within my wardrobe.

4. **Category size was unequal.** I desperately wanted more layering tops during the challenge period. With only 6 tops and 1 dress (worn as a top) included in my challenge wardrobe as the layering pieces, I often found myself with a laundry bottleneck because all of the tops would be dirty within the same week.

5. **Favorite outfits are repeated often, regardless of wardrobe size.** I had 15 bottoms in my challenge wardrobe, which meant that I would only be able to wear each bottom twice within the 30-day challenge period. Yet I found myself quickly reaching for the same handful of bottoms again and again, despite having more options. Apparently if I wanted to repeat bottoms more often than twice a month, I would need to own less items overall in my wardrobe.

6. **Preplanned outfits help on rush days.** Concerned with the small size of my challenge wardrobe, I brainstormed a number of outfit combinations at the start of the wardrobe challenge period. Having a collection of preplanned outfit combinations

was a real life saver on those days when there was no time, or I was simply too tired, to assemble a new outfit combination. If I want to dress quickly on a daily basis then I have to have a collection of preplanned outfits.

7. **I don't remix often.** My wardrobe threshold was relatively low when it came to remixing favorite outfits and fairly high for repeating favorite outfits. Apparently I do enjoy remixing wardrobe items into more than one outfit combination, but I don't enjoy remixing my clothes into endless combinations. I discover the 1 or 2 options that I like best, and then happily repeat them often.

Overall, I found this challenge was great for helping to push the envelope with my comfort zone regarding the size of my wardrobe. At the time I did this challenge, I still had a lot of clothes in my closet, I was struggling with deciding how many clothes I should own to be happy with what I had, and I wasn't convinced that limiting my extensive wardrobe down to a mere 30 or so pieces was really going to be fun or make me happy. In the beginning I struggled to do this challenge. I felt like a parent who loved all of their children, and now someone was asking me to pick a favorite out of the group. An impossible request. Despite the rough start, at the end I walked away excited and felt like I had just discovered the key to happiness with one's wardrobe—you don't need to own a *lot* of clothes, just the *right combination* of clothes. I also became curious, if I could be happy with using only a few of my clothes, how would I feel about trying to use *all* of them?

Wardrobe challenge #2—
Wear as much as you can

In complete contrast to the last challenge, where the wardrobe was limited to a small number of items, frequency challenges focus on using as much of your wardrobe as possible during the challenge period. If you are someone looking for a challenge that requires no set-up period, followed by a long challenge period, then this is the challenge for you. I participated in 2 frequency challenges—Wear It All, Not Once, But Twice and The 80/20 Wardrobe Challenge—here's what happened for both challenges.

Case study—Wear It All, Not Once, But Twice

The plan: As the title suggests, pick a start and end date, then attempt to wear everything in the wardrobe within that time period. I selected 1 year, but any time frame will work.

The wardrobe: In this challenge, it is very important to track the frequency of wearing clothing items. One option is to record everything one owns (either by hand or in an electronic spreadsheet) and then mark how often something is worn. A second tracking method is to flip all the hangers on the closet rod so that they face the wrong way. Items that are worn get the hanger flipped to the proper direction.

I walked away from this challenge with 3 key insights about my personal preferences:

1. **I finally figured out what I don't use.** This challenge highlights the wardrobe items that are not in use, allowing me to successfully purge the unworn items from my closet. By taking the time to identify what I really did and didn't use, I was able to prevent purging regret.

2. **Wardrobes may not have to accommodate the seasons equally.** I always knew that my wardrobe spanned multiple temperature ranges, and it was easy to acknowledge that a sweater will only be worn during cold months while a pair of shorts will only be used during hot weather. However, I never realized how unequal the use of season-specific items was for me. Living in a 4-season climate, I anticipated roughly 3 months for each season. Yet I found myself sporting fall and spring weight clothing in summer months (and even the occasional winter weight cardigan) due to my constant presence in air conditioned settings. I need to own a variety of clothing to cover 4 seasons, but the distribution of clothing is skewed towards owning more cold, rather than warm, weather items.

3. **Season-specific items sit for the majority of the year.** The hot weather season in my area runs for only 3 months. And within those 3 months, I am only able to sport shorts on weekends. If I wear my shorts on both days of the weekend, I'm able to wear them 8 times within 1 month. If I own 2 pairs of shorts, and wear each pair only once per weekend, that's only 4 times within 1 month, or 12 times for the entire season. In sharp contrast, a pair of blue skinny jeans that I only wear *once per week*, but I use for all 4 seasons, will get worn 52 times in a given year. Clearly my seasonal items get less use, because the weather in my area changes often.

When I began this challenge, I already knew I could get along just fine with using less than I owned, and the scientist in me was curious, if less equaled more happiness, would more do the exact opposite? I am happy to report that this experiment, ahem, I mean wardrobe challenge, was a success. The more I owned, the less I wanted to have. I walked away from this wardrobe challenge wanting to further reduce the size of my wardrobe, which led to the wardrobe refinement strategies discussed in Chapter 4 and ultimately helped me to design a wardrobe that I loved. Once I had my wardrobe at what I thought was the right size for me, I confirmed if I had the correct number by participating in the next wardrobe challenge.

The plan: Pick start and end dates then attempt to sport 80% of your wardrobe items regularly, leaving only 20% of items for the rarely used occasions. The 80% clothing category consists of items worn throughout the season, regularly. Regular use is defined as at least 2 times per month for the given season. The 20% clothing category consists of the capsules that are not frequently used (special occasion, formal business, etc) and items that are worn infrequently throughout a season. Over the challenge period, clothes are donated or discarded until 80% of the wardrobe is used often. The length of time for the challenge can vary; I selected 1 year. After a time frame has been selected, these are the 3 ground rules:

1. **Identify how many capsules you own and how much stuff is inside each one during month 1.** For every subsequent month, evaluate how often you are using your clothes within each capsule. Aim to wear 80% of your daily use capsule. For example, if it's the fall/winter season, strive to wear 80% of your fall/winter clothes throughout the month.

2. **Reevaluate every month to assess how frequently items are used.** For every month that you are not using 80% of your wardrobe, make adjustments by removing clothes and/or wearing more clothes during the next month. The challenge is over when you've reached the end date and/or you are using 80% of your wardrobe.

3. **One in/one out new purchases.** If an item cannot be designated for purging/donation, a new item can't be purchased.

The wardrobe: One's entire wardrobe is used in this challenge. As with prior challenges, I didn't include my outerwear or undergarment capsules. My challenge wardrobe contained 6 capsules: fall/winter (65 items), spring/summer (57 items), shoes (17 items), business/special occasion (14 items), beach/swim (8 items), and lounge/sleep (12 items).

I walked away from this challenge with 3 key insights about my personal preferences:

1. **Capsule size does not indicate frequency of use.** One of my smallest capsules was lounge/sleep, yet this capsule was used daily. One would anticipate that a capsule with items worn daily should have the most garments in it, but this is not always the case. That is because the size of a capsule is not correlated to the frequency of use the amount of repetition for each item coupled with the frequency of use, dictates the size of a wardrobe capsule. My lounge/sleep capsule was able to remain small despite its high frequency of use, because I repeat wearing the same outfit multiple times before washing. If I washed my lounge and sleepwear after every time I sported the item, then yes, this capsule would need to be larger in size. But, I only wear

these pieces for a few hours per day, so there was no need to wash them after each wear.

2. **Rarely used capsules should be small in number.** The size of rarely used capsules has to remain small, since these items will take up the bulk of the clothing that remains unworn for most of the year. The challenge wardrobe contained 173 items. To use 80% of this wardrobe only 35 items should sit unworn. However, this is across seasons. Let's take a closer look at how this fares for one of the seasons. For the fall/winter season, I had 65 fall/winter wardrobe items and 4 pairs of boots for a total of 69 items. This meant that for 20% of my fall/winter capsule to sit unused, only 14 items can sit unworn for the entire season. However, to make this slightly more complicated, I also had 22 items (business/special occasion capsule and beach/swim capsule items) that sit unworn for most of the year. Out of 173 items, these 22 items make up 12.7% already! That left me with only 12 items that should sit unworn between both my fall/winter *and* spring/summer capsule wardrobes, or 6 items each. That's not a lot of unworn clothes.

3. **Seasonal items often sit unworn—again.** The less seasonal items in a wardrobe, the fewer pieces that will sit unworn throughout the year. This challenge was the second time I noticed that season-specific items sit unworn for the majority of the year and

I began to shy away from buying these types of pieces for the future.

This challenge was great because it confirmed that the size of my wardrobe was the right size for me. Everything I owned I used at a rate that made me happy. With these first few challenges focused on the size of my wardrobe, I was ready to tackle a new angle—flexibility and versatility of my wardrobe.

Wardrobe challenge #3—
Wear as many combinations as you can

The heart of the remixing challenge is to test the flexibility and versatility of one's wardrobe. Remixing challenges focus on using a small subset of clothing—a capsule wardrobe—and then attempting to create as many individual outfits as possible from these pieces. While any capsule wardrobe can be used, often it is French (or Parisian) capsule wardrobes that are highlighted for these challenges. The classic elements of French style (timeless pieces and easy to remix core colors) lend themselves well to inspiration for remixing challenges. If you are looking for a challenge that enables you to create a capsule wardrobe, or you are interested in testing how cohesive your wardrobe is, then this is the challenge for you. I participated in 2 flexibility challenges—French Capsule Challenge and Play Tag Challenge. Here's what happened for both challenges.

The plan: Select a small number of items and a few colors to assemble as many different outfits as possible during the challenge period.

The wardrobe: I selected 21 items and originally desired only 3 colors for 3 weeks. Shoes were included in the challenge wardrobe, but outerwear and undergarments were not. I wanted to select 3 colors: white, black, and blue for clothing items. However, I didn't have a cobalt blue blazer, so I added in my next brightest colored blazer, which was kelly green. That left me with 4 colors for clothing items, although the bulk of the items were still white, black, and blue. Table 11 is the challenge wardrobe:

Table 11: *French Capsule Challenge Wardrobe—21 Items*

Toppers (4)	Tops (8)	Bottoms (5)	Dress (1)	Shoes (3)
Black Blazer	Black T-shirt	White Straight Leg Jeans	Black/White/Cobalt Print Dress	Black Flip Flops
Black Cardigan	White/Black Flower Print Top	White Bootcut Jeans		Black Ballet Flats
White Blazer	Black/White Abstract Print Top	Black Skinny Jeans		Gray Wedges
Kelly Green Blazer	White Cable Knit Top	Blue Bootcut Jeans		
	White/Black Dot Print Shirt	Cobalt Straight Leg Jeans		
	Black Bow Blouse			
	Cobalt Flower Print Tank			
	Black Print T-shirt			

I walked away from this challenge with 6 key insights about my personal preferences:

1. **No one else notices outfit repeats.** Working with such a small number of clothes meant I was repeating items more often. And usually in the same handful of combinations. Once I discovered a combination that I enjoyed, I tended to stick with it instead of continuing to try to remix the items in the outfit. Despite the repetition, the only one who seemed to notice that I was repeating items was me. At least no one ever said anything to me about it.

2. **A workable wardrobe is unnoticeable.** I really completed 4 weeks for the challenge, despite the fact that it was only supposed to go for 3 weeks, and I didn't realize it until I went back and counted the weeks! When I spend a morning frustrated with assembling an outfit, I spend the entire day thinking about how to fix it. Shall I shop for something new? Should I revisit my closet after work and try out new combinations? During the challenge, I didn't give my wardrobe a second thought. I felt that I had plenty of clothes that were easy for me to assemble into a variety of outfits.

3. **Fewer clothes and colors = faster dressing.** As expected, the fewer options I had, the less thinking I did for assembling an outfit, and the faster I got dressed. I never had a day of tossing piece after piece onto the bed or floor because I could not assemble an outfit.

4. **The same color across categories makes remixing easy.** Owning the same color *across all categories* makes remixing into new outfit combinations easy. It's like playing paper dolls for grown-ups. With only 2 colors, black and white, for all 3 categories (toppers, tops, and bottoms) I was able to assemble the following 8 outfits from only 6 items: black blazer, black t-shirt, black jeans, white blazer, white cable knit top, and white jeans:

Three-Item Outfit Formula: Topper + Top + Bottom

Outfit #1: Black Blazer + White Cable Knit Top + Black Jeans

Outfit #2: Black Blazer + Black T-shirt + Black Jeans

Outfit #3: Black Blazer + White Cable Knit Top + White Jeans

Outfit #4: Black Blazer + Black T-shirt + White Jeans

Outfit #5: White Blazer + White Cable Knit Top + Black Jeans

Outfit #6: White Blazer + Black T-shirt + Black Jeans

Outfit #7: White Blazer + White Cable Knit Top + White Jeans

Outfit #8: White Blazer + Black T-shirt + White Jeans

5. **Repetition within a category leads to wardrobe favorites.** On the flip side, owning the same color *within the same categories* was unnecessary duplication. I preferred to repeat only one of the options again and again, instead of sporting both items with equal frequency. Despite owning a black cardigan and a black blazer, I reached for the black blazer most often. When presented with both white

straight leg jeans *and* white bootcut jeans, I only selected the bootcut option (Table 12).

Table 12: *Frequency of Use for Garments of the Same Color Within the Same Category*

Toppers	Tops	Bottoms	Times Worn
Black Cardigan	Cobalt Flower Print Tank	Cobalt Straight Leg Jeans	1
Black Blazer	Black/White Abstract Print Top	Blue Bootcut Jeans	8
Black Blazer	White/Black Flower Print Top	Blue Bootcut Jeans	4
White Blazer	White/Black Dot Print Shirt	Cobalt Straight Leg Jeans	3
White Blazer	Black T-shirt	White Straight Leg Jeans	0
White Blazer	White/Black Dot Print Shirt	White Bootcut Jeans	4
Kelly Green Blazer	Black Bow Blouse	Black Skinny Jeans	5
Kelly Green Blazer	White Cable Knit Top	Cobalt Straight Leg Jeans	3

6. **Too many choices causes anxiety.** My challenge wardrobe, which contained far less clothing than what was in my closet at the time, made me happy. This was a sharp contrast to how I felt right before I started the challenge, when I had my entire wardrobe at my disposal. The large size and variety always left me feeling anxious, unsure of what to do with it all. My daily anxiety stemmed from what Barry Schwartz would call the "Paradox of Choice."[12] The more choices inside my closet, the less I knew what to do with it all. Having choice is crucial to feel freedom and to express creativity. But when it came to my wardrobe, I had too many options. Instead of feeling like I could soar, the daily anxiety about

[12] Schwartz B. *The Paradox of Choice: Why More Is Less*. New York: Ecco. 2004.

my wardrobe weighed me down. Even though I had previously done wardrobe challenges where I used a small number of clothes, this challenge wardrobe was the smallest one I had ever done, a mere 21 pieces, and I spent a large portion of time during this challenge in a state of awe at how much clothing that I owned, yet how little it took for me to be happy—again.

This is my favorite wardrobe challenge and I've completed it multiple times when I was working to reduce the size of my overall wardrobe. With this challenge I learned how to create a wardrobe capsule based on colors and proved to myself that I not only could survive my daily life using less clothes than I owned, but in doing so I was also really happy about it.

Less clothes = more happiness.

Intrigued by the ability to remix a small number of clothes again, and again, and again, I moved on to the next challenge to test just how versatile 1 garment of clothing could really be.

Case study—Play Tag Challenge

The plan: Similar to the game of tag, select one garment to act as the foundation from which all outfits will be built upon. Any garment can be used as the starting point.

The wardrobe: I chose my basic (the garment I tag) and then built as many outfits as I could around that item before selecting another basic to start with. For example, my blue denim shirt. My standard outfit was always to pair the denim shirt with a long sleeved T-shirt underneath (for added warmth) and a pair of black trousers for a fall look. During the challenge I discovered 3 additional outfits with the denim shirt:

1. **Denim shirt** + Gray long-sleeved T-shirt + Black trousers (original outfit)
2. Black sleeveless dress + **Denim shirt**
3. Ivory/Black print cardigan + **Denim shirt** + Dark blue skinny jeans
4. White lace panel knit + **Denim shirt** + Blue bootcut jeans

I walked away from this challenge with 3 key insights about my personal preferences:

1. **Basics really are wardrobe workhorses.** Often cited as the key component for minimal and highly versatile wardrobes, basics are those pieces that don't stand out in an outfit, instead they are the heavy lifters of a look. Wardrobe basics are the timeless pieces that can be paired with anything in a wardrobe. Blue skinny jeans, black straight leg trousers (or jeans), a white button-down shirt, a black or white T-shirt, a striped T-shirt, a denim jacket (or shirt), a black turtleneck, a black dress (or skirt), etc. These pieces let the trendy items shine in a look. However, because basics are the support cast, they are not usually the fun to shop for pieces and their utility is often overlooked. It can become

easy to dress in a rut, sporting the same basic with the same trendy item, again and again. Playing tag with a wardrobe basic unlocks the flexibility of what is otherwise considered a boring wardrobe item. Referring back to the denim shirt example above, I discovered that my denim shirt was easier to remix than I had originally planned at the time of purchase.

2. **Remixing 4 times was enough variety for me.** A wardrobe basic can be remixed into many outfit combinations, so why was my remixing number topping out at 4? Well, there are 4 weeks in a month, and I do laundry once a week. If I can assemble 4 outfits with my basic, I'll be able to sport that same piece once per week, for a month, reaffirming its place as an essential item for my wardrobe. Every time I attempted to move beyond 4, I immediately retreated back to reaching for 1 of the 4 established outfit combinations. I had found the 4 combinations that I enjoyed, and didn't need to go past that point.

3. **A garment can be layered in 2 ways.** While most wardrobe challenges involve a certain level of remixing an item, there are really only 2 ways to layer a garment in an outfit—top or bottom. When an item is the top layer, it's the piece that you see the most in an outfit. Once again going back to the denim shirt example from above, the denim shirt was worn 2 ways—as the top layer, with

additional items layered underneath (gray long-sleeved T-shirt or black sleeveless dress) and as the bottom layer, with less of the denim shirt visible in the outfit (underneath the white lace panel knit or underneath the ivory/black print cardigan). By rotating between layering an item as the top or the bottom layer, the versatility of a piece is greatly expanded. Also, wardrobe boredom is lessened because I'm no longer wearing the same item in the same exact combination every time.

Before this wardrobe challenge I always thought shopping for basics was boring and I would shy away from doing so. And then I would struggle to assemble an outfit in the morning and not understand why I was having a problem. The solution was simple—own more basics! After finishing this wardrobe challenge I began to add more basic pieces to my closet and it has drastically improved my ability to get dressed in the mornings. Shopping for wardrobe basics may not be a lot of fun, but basics are a crucial component of a well-functioning wardrobe.

And speaking of having a little fun, the next wardrobe challenge is probably at the top of the list to do just that.

Wardrobe challenge #4—
Dress based on an image or key word

With an inspirational challenge, the focus is on using an image or key word as the starting point for your outfit. Photographs, pictures, book or album covers, statues or figurines, celebrities, logos, and artwork are all great starting points for an inspiration-based challenge. If you are looking for a challenge that enables you to think outside the box, test how flexible your wardrobe is (or isn't), or you are simply looking for a challenge that lasts only 1 day, then this is the challenge for you. Here's what happened when I participated in the wardrobe challenge.

Case study—Dress Like a Daisy Flower

The plan: Select an image as a starting point, then create an outfit inspired by the image using 1 of the 3 options: colors, textures, or emotions.

The wardrobe: I chose the daisy flower as my inspiration image. Color is the easiest and most literal interpretation for this challenge. I created an outfit that paired together the same color combinations that are used in the image. For the image of a daisy, I paired together white, yellow, and a little green into my outfit. I sported a white top, yellow trousers, and a green bracelet. A second option would be to use textures, which focus on the physical elements of the image. Using the white daisy example again, I could sport a button-down shirt (which echoes the smooth petals on the daisy) with a pair of corduroy trousers (a nod to the texture of the daisy's disc florets, the yellow center of the daisy). The third and broadest interpretation of the image would be to use emotions. Returning to the white daisy example once more, this flower always makes me smile and feel happy. As a nod to the joy I have with daisies I could simply sport an outfit that makes me happy to wear for the day.

I walked away from this challenge with 2 key insights about my personal preferences:

1. **My wardrobe has lots of flexibility.** As I've mentioned from previous challenges, I am a fan of repeating the same outfit combinations often. But the ability to assemble my wardrobe into an outfit based on an image demonstrates that there's always a new way to wear my clothes, if I'm open to doing so.

2. **Accessories help complete a look, when I remember them.** During this challenge I found the use of accessories was helpful to tie together an outfit. I often forget about accessories when I shop and dress for the day. I've performed a few inspiration challenges since the daisy one, and every time, it's been the accessories—a printed scarf, a suede handbag, a piece of jewelry—that completed my outfit and provided the tie in to the inspiration image that I was searching for.

This is my second favorite wardrobe challenge. It's fast and easy to do, and it gets me to think outside of the box. Inspiration is all around us, and it helps to get me out of my comfort zone with my wardrobe when I get into a dressing rut. If you are in a rut with how you get dressed every day, the next challenge should help you shake things up a bit.

Wardrobe challenge #5—
Give favorite outfit formulas a "time out"

This wardrobe challenge zeroes in on your favorite outfit formula, then tweaks it to freshen up your look while still keeping in line with your personal style. If you've been sporting the same outfit formula for years and it's starting to feel a little dull and uninspiring, then this is the challenge for you. Sometimes the best way to cool off a heated conversation is to take a time out, give both parties a chance to take a breather and regroup their thoughts and ideas. The same thing can be done with your wardrobe. Here's what happened when I put my favorite outfit formula in a "time out."

The plan: As the challenge says, pick a favorite outfit formula, then change 1 item in the formula to freshen up the look

The wardrobe: For years I adored the formula of:

Boots + Jeans + Blazer + Scarf = BJBS

I kept the preference of sporting a layered look for this challenge by putting my blazers in "time out" and sporting cardigans instead. The new outfit formula was:

Boots + Jeans + Cardigan + Scarf = BJCS

Alternatively I could have replaced the scarf for statement necklaces, the boots for flat or heeled shoes, or the jeans for trousers. The simple swap of a blazer for a cardigan freshened up the outfit formula, without forcing me to steer away from the layered looks that I adore.

I walked away from this challenge with 1 key insight about my personal preferences:

1. **Tweaking an outfit formula prevents wardrobe repetition.** The BJBS formula was easy for me to change as the seasons passed, simply swap the materials and colors for year-round use, and it's the key reason why I wore this outfit formula as often as I did. A black tall leather boot for the fall was swapped with a chestnut cowboy boot for spring. A wool scarf for the winter was replaced with a linen option during the summer months. Constantly wearing the same outfit eventually led me to overshop for wardrobe pieces that fit the BJBS formula. The BJBS formula was always at the top of my mind, therefore I quickly amassed over a dozen blazers and jeans, added more than 20 scarves, and accumulated 8 pairs of boots. Sporting a BJBS outfit had become a habit, and the familiarity of an outfit formula that worked prevented me from searching for any items that didn't fit into the formula. But I grew bored. Adding new styles of blazers and boots no longer satisfied my wardrobe boredom. Adjusting the formula from BJBS to BJCS helped to freshen up my look, and I was also able to increase the variety in my wardrobe.

If I had never put the original BJBS outfit formula on hold, I would have continued to add more and more and more of the same pieces, causing my wardrobe to creep up in size. I would have continued to function with the misguided belief that adding a new color or material of yet another blazer would end my wardrobe boredom. But it was adding a new style of topper, not a greater number, which helped to reinvigorate my wardrobe and to end wardrobe creep.

I revisit this wardrobe challenge 4 times per year, typically in the middle of each season. Usually by that time, I've worn my regular outfit combinations a handful of times already and I'm starting to feel like my daily dressing mimics that of a robot, mindlessly grabbing the same outfit formula every single day. Periodically swapping out an item to mix up the outfit formula keeps me from getting into a dressing rut and helps to stave off boredom with my wardrobe, which in turn prevents me from going out mid-season to shop for something new to freshen up my look. Instead I'm able to save my money so that I can shop for the upcoming season instead. If I'm still feeling restless in the middle of a season and I want another wardrobe challenge to do, or I'm just plain ol'stuck with how to put together a capsule wardrobe, I'll participate in the next wardrobe challenge.

Wardrobe challenge #6—
Unlock the power of 2

The majority of the wardrobe challenges in this chapter have one thing in common: they require you to assemble a wardrobe using a small portion of your stuff. The challenge wardrobe is limited by either the number of garments or the style and colors included; in essence, you are asked to work with a capsule wardrobe. When I first attempted to perform a wardrobe challenge, I struggled to get past the starting point, putting together the challenge wardrobe itself. I didn't know how to create a capsule wardrobe and I was confused as to what pieces I would need to create outfits. I was stuck.

In order to create a capsule wardrobe, you have to know what your color pairings (or total number of items) are going to be and you have to know how to assemble an outfit. The final wardrobe challenge in this chapter—The Power of 2 Challenge— zeroes in on this problem because you will work with a small number of colors, or items, to help you figure out how to create outfit combinations. When you want to participate in a wardrobe challenge but you can't figure out where to begin to create a wardrobe capsule, you want to practice building and/or remixing outfits around a central color or item, or you are simply looking for another challenge to do, these are the challenges for you. I participated in 2 The Power of 2 Challenges—2-*color* remix challenge and 2-*item* remix challenge. Here's what happened for both challenges.

Case study—2-color remix challenge

The plan: Select 2 colors from your wardrobe then rotate as many outfit combinations as possible built around these 2 colors before having to add a third color. The 2-color remix challenge demonstrates how well clothes of specific colors do (or do not) remix with each other.

The wardrobe: My 2 colors were black and white. I began with 4 items: black top, white top, black bottoms, white bottoms. I always begin with 4 outfits: rotating the colors for the first 2 outfits followed by sporting a column of color to assemble the last 2 outfits. For example:

Outfit #1: Black top + White bottoms

Outfit #2: White top + Black bottoms

Outfit #3: Black top + Black bottoms

Outfit #4: White top + White bottoms

With the first 4 outfit combinations under my belt, I'll then add a fifth piece, usually a print that contains both colors. To ensure I've created all combinations possible with the fifth addition, I pair every bottom with every top. For example, using the black and white colors, I added a black and white stripe blouse to include 2 more outfits:

Outfit #5: Black and white stripe blouse + White bottoms

Outfit #6: Black and white stripe blouse + Black bottoms

If the print has a third (or even fourth color) in it, then those become the new colors I continue to build my capsule wardrobe around. For example, if I also add a black/white/cobalt abstract print knit, I will now want to add a third color to my mix—cobalt. I can add 6 new outfits by adding only 2 pieces: a print knit with cobalt and a pair of cobalt bottoms:

Outfit #7: Black/White/Cobalt abstract print knit + Black bottoms

Outfit #8: White top + Cobalt bottoms

Outfit #9: Black top + Cobalt bottoms

Outfit #10: Black/White/Cobalt abstract print knit + White bottoms

Outfit #11: Black and white stripe blouse + Cobalt bottoms

Outfit #12: Black/White/Cobalt Abstract print knit + Cobalt bottoms

I walked away from this challenge with 3 key insights about my personal preferences:

1. **It doesn't take a lot to generate variety.** With only 7 items (4 tops [black top, white top, black and white stripe blouse, black/white/cobalt abstract print knit], 3 bottoms [black, white, and cobalt]), I was able to assemble 12 outfits, almost 2 full weeks of variety.

2. **For maximum remixing of outfit combinations, own colors that pair well together.** When a wardrobe is very cohesive, many of the items pair well with each other and can be remixed in lots of combinations, without using a lot of individual pieces. With my challenge wardrobe I was able to

easily remix my clothes because the pairing of black and white is appealing to my eye.

3. **Columns of color outfits lead to greater remixing potential.** Two outfits that are a column of color automatically generate 4 outfit combinations, as demonstrated by the all-white and all-black outfits mentioned earlier. Even if I don't want to wear an outfit that is head-to-toe only one color, owning an outfit of this style makes remixing clothes easier.

This challenge has not only helped keep wardrobe boredom away, it has also streamlined my shopping habits. From this challenge I've discovered what my favorite color pairings and I have used this knowledge to help decide what prints to buy when I go shopping for something new. I've also learned that I don't enjoy remixing more than 3 colors together into an outfit; therefore, I seek out printed items as well as solid color pieces that will let me easily pair together an outfit with only 3 colors. The next challenge helped further reinforce that I enjoy dressing with a specific number in mind, and for me that number is 3.

*Case study—2-**item** remix challenge*

The plan: This time instead of selecting 2 colors, select 2 items and build outfits around those 2 pieces, remixing as much as possible. The 2 chosen items don't have to pair well with each other. The 2-item remix challenge is an exercise on how to create an outfit, with the starting point of 1 item.

The wardrobe: Similar to the previous challenge, I selected 2 items, then rotated many outfit combinations built around these 2 pieces.

I walked away from this challenge with 2 key insights about my personal preferences:

1. **A small wardrobe has very few outlier pieces.** Outlier wardrobe items are those pieces that don't remix well with the rest of your closet. It's perfectly fine to own outlier items; however, if I'm seeking to own a small wardrobe, I may not want to own lots of outlier pieces, because these clothes will not remix easily. For example, my challenge items were 2 pieces that don't pair well with each other for an outfit—camo printed jeans and a kelly green blazer. Not only do these items not pair well with each other, but also these are 2 pieces that I always struggle to style into *any* outfit. I began with the camo printed jeans, pairing them with as many of my wardrobe basics as possible, focusing on the solids as they often can pair well with any print or color. Using 5 garments (black knit, white shirt, black blazer, denim shirt, and coral hoodie) I was able to create 4 outfits with the camo printed jeans:

Outfit #1: Black Knit + **Camo Printed Jeans**

Outfit #2: White Shirt + **Camo Printed Jeans**

Outfit #3: Black Blazer + Denim Shirt + **Camo Printed Jeans**

Outfit #4: Coral Hoodie + **Camo Printed Jeans**

After I exhausted the combinations of items I could pair with my camo printed jeans, I tried out all of these combinations with my second challenge item, the kelly green blazer. Since the blazer is a topper, only the layering items from above would pair with the blazer here. I also added 3 bottoms, to complete the looks:

Outfit #5: Black Knit + **Kelly Green Blazer** + White Jeans

Outfit #6: White Shirt + **Kelly Green Blazer** + Black Jeans

Outfit #7: Denim Shirt + **Kelly Green Blazer** + Blue Jeans

With only 2 outlier items, I was able to generate 7 different outfits. However, to do so I had to include an additional 8 pieces! That's 10 items for only 7 outfits, a sharp contrast to the last challenge where I was able to create 12 outfits with only 7 items. The more statement oriented the clothing is, the harder it will be to remix the item into new outfit combinations.

2. **I prefer outfits with a third piece to elevate the look.** I adored both of the items I selected for this challenge. However, I preferred the outfits with the kelly green blazer over the camo printed jeans. Why? The blazer outfits all consisted of 3 pieces, while most of the jeans outfits were only 2 items. Outfits with a layered look often have more visual interest, and for my personal style, I preferred the outfits where the third piece added an extra detail. Moving forward I always take note of what third item is adding interest to my outfits. I elevate my

outfits by layering blazers, cardigans, pullovers, and scarves over thin-weight knits, blouses, shirts, and T-shirts in the winter months. When it's hot outside I sport a light-weight scarf, a vest, or a tank top as my third piece to maintain a layered look in the heat.

These 2 wardrobe challenges demonstrated to me that I not only enjoy outfits with 3 colors, but also 3 items. With this knowledge I began to shop with layered outfits in mind, to support my personal preference for looks containing the number 3.

Overall, unlocking The Power of 2 is not only a great way to jump-start a wardrobe challenge, it's also a useful exercise to learn how versatile something you just bought is going to be when added to your wardrobe. If I can only remix my new purchase with the rest of the items in my wardrobe into 1 or 2 looks, I may want to return it for something better suited for my wardrobe.

Wardrobe challenges can be a lot of fun, and they will also provide some great insight into how you think and use the pieces in your wardrobe. The number one insight that I discovered regardless of which challenge I participated in was:

To be happy with my wardrobe, I don't need to own a *lot* of clothes, just the *right combination* of clothes.

Wardrobe challenges help to keep your wardrobe feeling fresh and interesting without having to shop for something new. As soon as I feel the urge to go shopping because I am bored or uninspired by what I own, I begin a wardrobe challenge. After all, the entire point of owning a closet full of clothes is to have a little fun with it.

Chapter 10 recap:

Don't forget to have fun with your wardrobe.

 Hit The Brakes:
Participate in a wardrobe challenge to have fun with your wardrobe

• Select one of the following challenges when you grow bored with your wardrobe:

1. **Limit items and days.** Wear a predetermined number of clothes (and sometimes shoes and accessories too) and use only that number for a prespecified length of time

2. **Wear as much as you can.** Select start and end dates, then use as much of your wardrobe as possible during the challenge period

3. **Wear as many combinations as you can.** Sport as many different outfits as you can during the challenge period

4. **Dress based on an image or key word.** Use an image or key word as the starting point for your outfit

5. **Give favorite outfit formulas a "time out."** Shift one item from a favorite item formula to freshen up your outfits

6. **Unlock the power of 2.** Practice creating outfits by selecting 2 colors or 2 wardrobe items, then assembling outfits with those colors (or pieces)

Take a break from analyzing, organizing, and shopping for your wardrobe by participating in a wardrobe challenge. Don't forget about the end goal of managing a wardrobe—to have a little fun with what you own.

Special Thanks

The final version of this book would not have been possible without the hard work and dedication of a talented group of people. I am grateful to have had the opportunity to work with them. I could never properly acknowledge everyone who has helped me in one way or another towards creating this book, but there are a few special people that I would like to thank. I want to thank my amazing beta reader Rachelle Oldmixon for not only helping me shape this work into something someone else can read, but for also being my Zen. Thank you to my eagle-eyed editor Kelly Hogate for smoothing out the rough edges and providing a listening ear at the times when I needed it the most. I also want to thank the incredibly talented Britta Nagy; it's been a blast collaborating with you as we worked to bring my creative ideas to life. To my little sister, Kiddo, this book is proof that if you dream it, you can make it happen. Never forget that.

Most of all, I want to thank my husband and soul mate. Every brainstorming session, every rough draft, every freak out session, you've been by my side with unwavering love and support through it all. Babe, you really are the best thing.

About The Author

Lisa Deerwood is a recovering shopaholic who has spent more than a decade studying shopping addiction and wardrobe management. She holds a Master's of Science in Biology, with a Molecular Biology concentration from Montclair State University, and currently lives in New Jersey with her husband and cat who does tricks for treats. Unwilling to sit still for long periods of time, when she is not writing she can be found lifting weights, practicing katas, riding horses, and managing her blog: shoppingbrake.com.

Made in the USA
Monee, IL
26 May 2021